THREE STUDIES IN
ENGLISH LITERATURE

THREE STUDIES
IN
ENGLISH LITERATURE

KIPLING, GALSWORTHY, SHAKESPEARE

By
ANDRE CHEVRILLON, 1864-1957.
(DE L'ACADÉMIE FRANÇAISE)

From the French by
FLORENCE SIMMONDS
OFFICIER D'ACADÉMIE

KENNIKAT PRESS, INC./PORT WASHINGTON, N. Y.

THREE STUDIES IN ENGLISH LITERATURE

First published in 1923
Reissued in 1967 by Kennikat Press

Library of Congress Catalog Card No: 67-27585
Manufactured in the United States of America

ESSAY AND GENERAL LITERATURE INDEX REPRINT SERIES

TRANSLATOR'S NOTE

THE translation of these three studies, the work of a distinguished Frenchman, whose knowledge of English letters and sympathy with English thought give him a place apart, even among the most brilliant of contemporary " anglicisants," has been a fascinating but not an easy task. Monsieur Chevrillon's style is so individual, his intellectual processes are so essentially French, that, as he himself declared, no passable English version of his book was to be hoped for without the close collaboration of the author. This, however, was most generously offered, and it has been my pleasant privilege to revise my work with Monsieur Chevrillon. A certain freedom in the rendering, which a translator could not have ventured upon independently, became, of course, legitimate under such supervision.

I am proud to acknowledge further the help of Monsieur Chevrillon's great colleague, Monsieur Bergson, in two difficult passages (pp. 196, 205). Monsieur Bergson was so kind as to explain these himself, and his version appears in footnotes by his permission, given with the smiling comment : " *Me voilà donc passé traducteur."* He added that he congratulated himself, as he considered " *l'art du traducteur comme l'un des plus delicats et difficiles* "—an appreciation very grateful to one who, perhaps with more courage than judgment, has made many essays in the all but impossible art.

F. S.

STOCKHOLM,
January, 1923.

CONTENTS

RUDYARD KIPLING'S POETRY

I.—YOUTHFUL INFLUENCES

KIPLING's poetry is but little known in France, and this is natural. It is hardly possible to translate poetry, for all its magic lies in the power and the order of certain words, chosen not only for the accents, rhythms and sonorities which appeal to the ear, but for the resonance each one awakens in the soul, the harmonics which vibrate in subtle modulations around the fundamental note. Only by a happy chance can those sections of the real for which the words of a language stand, correspond exactly to those represented by the words of another tongue. Such coincidence is rare indeed in the case of two idioms like French and English, the one so analytic and clarified that it compels clear thinking, the other so rich in evocative symbols, and with such power to express the lingering echoes of emotion. When, moreover, it is a question of English poetry, where such magic words predominate, the task may well seem hopeless.

This is doubtless why so little of this poetry—great though it be—has been able to thrive in France. We may add that it is, above all, poetry of the soul, of an insular soul, shaped by moral influences, governed by a system of discipline, directed towards an ideal other

1

than ours. Broadly speaking, it would seem that of all the works of English literature, those accepted on the Continent are the least specifically English and the most universal, those which respond to sympathies, yearnings and passions common to all men. A Byron, whose spirit of revolt stimulated that of the French romantic school, a Scott, whose pictures of the Middle Ages harmonised with our tendency to forget ourselves in visions of the past, a Dickens, who spoke to all kindly hearts, were accepted on our side of the Channel; but not a Wordsworth, nor truly a Ruskin, too Puritan in his inspiration, nor even a George Eliot nor a Thackeray, whose characters are too essentially of the Island. We know little of Wells' satiric studies of English types and manners; but who has not read his stories of other worlds ? Martians and Selenites are interesting to all Terrestrials. And so with Kipling's East—the deep unchanging East—which appeals to the imagination of all men of the West. But his poetry is purely and strongly English.

We must, however, attempt to give some idea of it, even if we confine ourselves to a mere outline of the themes. Not only does the poetic work of this master extend over the third of a century, not only does it run parallel to the whole of his prose work, so much of which, like the *Arabian Nights*, enchants men of all races, but it is closely bound up with the life of England throughout this eventful period ; it follows or foretells its great moments, its crises and dangers ; it seems the direct expression of this life in the course of all these years, of its triumphs, presentiments, anxieties and anguish—for such was the process of history. From the beginning, towards 1890, it is obviously directed by a foreboding of the event towards which the world was darkly moving.

In 1919, Rudyard Kipling, who for the last fifteen years had given the public no collection of really new verse,[1] gathered together the latest and, perhaps, most moving part of his poetical work;[2] and a few weeks later he brought out a complete edition in a single volume. It was like a new discovery when just after the war the poems of a life-time appeared, linked together and borne out each by each. In the first place, the fulfilment of fate had given them new values and significance. Many marvelled that Kipling should have foreseen and foretold the danger so far back, and were amazed at his certitude, his persistent, insistent divination; they talked of a gift of second sight—less surprising to those who recalled the visionary faculty, the power of the *vates*, already revealed in many of the writer's prose inventions. Especially in the fading glow of the flames which had just devastated Europe and had been so close a threat to England, the general meaning of the work stood out clearly. Englishmen recognised its continuity, its logic, its growing fervour as *The Day* drew nearer—all its practical vital value to England and the English race at large. They realised that in the soul whence this poetry had flowed the life of a

---

[1] The *Songs from Books* (Toronto, 1912 ; London, 1913), a collection of the songs scattered throughout his books, were not new to readers of Kipling's tales.

[2] *The Years Between* (London, 1919).

certain human family, its consciousness of itself, were reflected and concentrated—also that it had never ceased to be passionately stirred by the adventures, efforts, triumphs and perils of the English tribe, and that its insight had doubtless been increased by this very passion. To Englishmen, Kipling might indeed appear as the poet of the English. And thus he had defined himself some twenty years earlier in symbolical language :

In the Neolithic Age savage warfare did I wage
For food and fame and woolly horses' pelt ;
I was singer to my clan in that dim red Dawn of
    Man,
And I sang of all we fought and feared and felt.

And after describing this mysterious former existence he added :

Then the silence closed upon me till They put new
    clothing on me
Of whiter, weaker flesh and bone more frail,
And I stepped beneath Time's finger, once again a
    tribal singer. . . .[1]

How does this singer reappear ? By what crossing of their threads do the Fates bring him back and adapt him to his clan of to-day—a clan scattered under all the skies of the world ? Of this we must form some idea. Poetry such as this, so varied in its unity, becomes more intelligible, we realise its significance better, not only

---

[1] *In the Neolithic Age* in *The Seven Seas.*

in the history of English literature, but in the history of England itself, when we know whence Kipling came, and the peculiar influences that shaped him.

He is an Englishman of the Empire, not of England. The light on which he first opened his eyes was that of India ; he was born at Bombay (1865) " between the palms and the sea." A strange nature and humanity enveloped him from the beginning. Imagine a little European boy, blanched by the hot-house moisture of the great Asiatic port. His home is some bungalow under the fringes of tall palms, among which parrots gleam, and fire-flies at the sudden fall of night float like slow, wandering stars. Like all Anglo-Indian children, he lives a good deal with the servants of the house, a hierarchy of Hindus and Musulmans, white robed and barefooted, so stately and ceremonious when they " *salaam*." Surely, there is a " bearer," with the red or yellow marks of Siva or Vishnu between his eyes, standing at meals behind the child's high chair, according to custom. There is also an *ayah*, one of those serious, tender Indian nurses (classic bronze features, bejewelled nostril, dusky velvet eyes), so ready to crouch in adoration before the little one—he may sing some day of those " dear dark foster mothers." From her lips he catches, and faster than he learns English from his mother's tongue, the words used by the naked babies of the bazaar, the songs about Shiv and Hari, the tales of the man-eater tiger, Shere Khan. For walks in the cooler hours there are the groves and avenues where the palms shoot up, green and smooth like giant weeds—and the beach where the flashing breakers dash themselves, where at sunrise and sunset the Parsees, standing in the scarlet waters, bow down before the God. Sometimes, at the swift Eastern daybreak (what a clamour among the gray crows when the city begins to stir under its veil of rosy mists !) he is taken to the wonderful fruit market. His *ayah* is a Catholic ; often on the way they will enter a porch surmounted by a cross, and kneel before the statue of Beebee Myriam (the Holy Virgin), which will not prevent them (such is India) from pausing a little further on at the shrine of some obese elephant-trunked Ganesh, and devoutly encircling his neck with a garland of marigolds. Thus, when only five years old, one little Anglo-Indian boy is at his ease in the midst of several religions, and mingling with the native crowd overhears their talk, full of a practical philosophy and simple wisdom, which at once initiates him, like Kim and most Indian children, into all that which in the West is so carefully veiled from the young. Later on he will be unable to remember when these mysteries were unknown to him. Here we have two factors which explain certain peculiarities in Kipling's work. His attitude towards the various religions and more obviously towards questions of sex is not that of his compatriots, and this somewhat scandalised the Islanders in years that still belonged to the Victorian age. They had yet to know him as the rigorous poet of Duty.

Doubtless the child learns other things at Bombay, which leave a lasting impression. He sees the fine soldiers of the Queen ; he sees the Sepoys presenting arms to the Europeans. He sees in the bazaars, around the temples and sacred ponds, the dark, half-naked crowd, making way for the Englishman's horse. He sees the *salaams*, the hands laid on heart, lips, and bending brow. Surely the child is aware that he belongs to the ruling race—his nurse or his bearer must have told him that he is a *sahib*. And maybe he has already formed some idea of the duties and the honour of a *sahib*.[1]

All this until he is six years old. The English have the sense of race, and the same instinct which forbids them to intermarry with the natives saves them from becoming Creoles. Their children are removed at an early age from tropical influences and are sent home to be hardened and trained, body and soul, in the cold air of England. What does this particular child see and understand of the voyage on the great P. and O. steamer which bears him away with many others of his age ? At first nothing but blue days, blue seas with flying fish, games on the deck, the cold gradually stealing in (it makes itself felt in the upper half of the Red Sea), and suddenly one morning the first turmoil of the North. A memory the poet will recall in one of his charming nursery songs :

When the cabin port-holes are dark and green
    Because of the seas outside ;
When the ship goes *wop* (with a wiggle between)
And the steward falls into the soup-tureen,
    And the trunks begin to slide ;

[1] *Wee Willie Winkie.*

7

When Nursey lies on the floor in a heap,
And Mummy tells you to let her sleep,
And you aren't waked or washed or dressed,
Why then you will know (if you haven't guessed)
You're " Fifty north and Forty west ! "

—and that England is near. Then all of a sudden, there it is ! A misty cliff standing stark against a wan sky, a ghostly, low shore, and further on, a beach with rows of dull houses, all alike, lifeless against the leaden background. How slowly the sun travels ! What a cold, cold sea ! Things look so miserable ! One little boy shivers. . . .

Then, five years of a somewhat sombre experience, which Dickens would have described in detail with his tender, sympathetic humour—which Kipling hints at briefly in the first pages of *The Light that Failed*. They are spent at Portsmouth, a place very different from Bombay ; more like our Brest—so gray, so rainy, so full of barracks. Ramparts, forts, cannon, war-ships, long bugle-calls, the clangour of the dockyard, dreary suburbs, distant waters growing dim and vanishing out in the fog ; also workmen, sailors, retired skippers, naval officers. . . . He lives with one of these, whose wife receives little boys from overseas. A strongly religious, rigid person of Puritan bent. One feels lonely with her in the evening—so far from one's mamma. So little love, and so much Bible ! It was here that the strong scriptural essence was instilled for life into the child who had twined garlands round monstrous Ganesh amidst Hindu throngs and

8

smells. What the influence of "the Book" will be on Kipling's poetry, on its vocabulary, movements and accents, may be seen later.

He is eleven years old now, the age at which an English boy passes into the hands of men, to be made a man. For children of his class this means nearly always a boarding-school; but let us not think in this connection of all that the term suggests to the French mind. The English school is in the country, often by the seaside; it has fields and playgrounds, to which the boys are not confined—the bounds may be a mile or two from the house. An English school is above all a rearing ground. Is the body of "man's cub" of less worth than that of a young horse?—the fulness of his natural powers of less value to himself, his country and race? But here the soul as well as the body is trained. By the stress it lays on religion, honour and morality; by its insistence on character; by its discipline and freedom, which make for self-control, self-government and self-reliance; by its compulsory games, which teach him to obey that he may learn to command; by the system that enlists the older boys on the side of order, and confers authority upon them; by its very punishments—those stripes which should be received without wincing; by its traditions of common life and activity—such a school aims at coining Englishmen of the true, standard type, healthy, steadfast men, capable of joy and action, spontaneously devoted to duty, firmly welded into the social group, and of distinct value to that group. The point of view here is practical—that of life rather than of knowledge, the life of the community, which a boy learns to serve whilst learning faithfulness to his daily work. Of such ideas, which everything in such schools fosters, young Kipling began to feel the influence at the age when the sap of life buds into thought. They permeated his growing mind, his soul, all of himself that was to come out later. From them he derived the ethics, nay, the very faith which is the ground-work of his poetry.

This school, so well adapted to the needs and instincts of youth, yet keeping it in such wholesome subjection to a manly discipline, left happy and lasting recollections. Its games, work, customs, joys, follies and graver aspects he has described at length in one of his novels. Its spirit he has expressed in a song—the *School Song*—dedicated to his former masters :

> " Let us now praise famous men "—
> Men of little showing—
> For their work continueth,
> And their work continueth,
> Broad and deep continueth,
> Greater than their knowing !
>
> Western wind and open surge
> Took us from our mothers,
> Flung us on a naked shore
> (Twelve bleak houses by the shore !
> Seven summers by the shore !)
> 'Mid two hundred brothers.
>
> There we met with famous men,
> Set in office o'er us ;

RUDYARD KIPLING

And they beat on us with rods—
Faithfully with many rods—
Daily beat on us with rods,
For the love they bore us.

     .   .   .   .   .   .

Each degree of latitude
Strung about Creation,
Seeth one or more of us,
(Of one muster each of us),
Diligent in that he knows,
Keen in his vocation.

This we learned from famous men,
Knowing not its uses,
When they showed, in daily work,
Man must finish off his work—
Right or wrong, his daily work,
And without excuses.

     .   .   .   .   .   .

This we learned from famous men,
Teaching in our borders,
Who declarèd it was best,
Safest, easiest and best—
Expeditious, wise and best—
To obey your orders.

Some beneath the further stars
Bear the greater burden ;
Set to serve the lands they rule,
(Save he serve no man may rule),
Serve and love the lands they rule,
Seeking praise nor guerdon.

This we learned from famous men,
Knowing not we learned it.

11

ENGLISH LITERATURE

> Only, as the years went by—
> Lonely, as the years went by—
> Far from help as years went by,
> Plainer we discerned it.[1]

How well this song reveals the guiding principle of
such a school : the awakening in young minds of the
social sense ! It tells us, moreover, of the special
character of this school, which was to play such a
part in the shaping of the poet. The majority of the
" two hundred brothers " had come like himself from
overseas. Each mail brought them letters from their
fathers—civil servants, administrators, officers—nearly
all entrusted with imperial tasks—tasks for which
their children were destined. Thus, they feel that far,
far away, beyond the horizon of the Islanders, beyond
the narrow limits of England, the land of enclosures,
all parcelled out and registered eight hundred years ago,
lie other spaces, continents where England's will and
action have penetrated, old Oriental worlds where it is
her mission to establish law and justice. Above all, they
accept that idea of service which was to become the
dominant strain in the poet of *The Five Nations*, the principle of his moral and social philosophy. Before Joseph

---

[1] It is obvious that the English school, as it appears in
this poem and in *Stalky & Co.*, is bound up with a social
system spontaneously developed in the course of time, in
which certain ideas prevail to the exclusion of others. A
civilisation, like all living forms, is an organic whole. The
English school cannot therefore be compared to the French
school, which forms part of a different system. In the
course of this study we may see something of the difference
of principle underlying the two cultures.

Chamberlain had uttered the word, they "thought imperially," as far as they thought at all.

But about the year 1880 Kipling is one of those who think. A poem he wrote at the age of sixteen shows the trend of his mind and the spirit of the school. He offers the homage of "Westward Ho!" to the Queen who had just escaped from the attempt of an assassin (March, 1882):

> Such greeting as should come from those
> Whose fathers faced the Sepoy hordes,
> Or served You in the Russian snows,
> And dying, left their sons their swords.
>
> And some of us have fought for You
> Already, in the Afghan pass,
> Or where the scarce-seen smoke-puffs flew
> From Boer marksmen in the grass,
>
> And all are bred to do Your will
> By land or sea—wherever flies
> Your flag to fight and follow still,
> And work Your Empire's destinies.

Let us mark this word "Empire" uttered by a school-boy. For the first time it is used in the sense it has retained on English lips since the appearance of Kipling's great popular poems. The verses were called *Ave Imperatrix*. Now that nearly forty years have passed the poet is convinced that there and then, under the influence of "Westward Ho!" the general direction of his life-work was determined.

Had he already some idea of this life-work? He was simply writing, writing for his own pleasure: sheaves of manuscript ! His masters were not without some inkling of the future ; it was plain that he was not like the others—that the world of representation was predominant with him. They took care not to tell him he was different—a poor compliment to an Englishman, the national system of education tending rather to suppress originality (*Of one muster each of us*). But so unmistakable was the gift that the Headmaster could not but feel an interest in it, though he refrained from comment and made no sign. On the plea that the young writer needed time and quiet for his editorship of the *School Journal*, he was excused from some of the compulsory games, and given free access to the Headmaster's library.

Here young Kipling read deeply and widely, slaking his intellectual thirst not only with the masters of his own tongue, especially those of the riotous English Renaissance, but with the French (he went straight to the giants : Rabelais, Balzac, Hugo), and even the great Russians. For he began the study of Russian early, urged thereto, no doubt, by his Anglo-Indian patriotism, by the old idea that the born enemy of British rule in India is the Muscovite. He proposed to watch the foe.

At the age of sixteen and a half, when his school life came to an end, he was given his choice : the university, as the traditional path to a liberal career in England, or India, which he had left ten years before. He chose India, and decided his fate. This early return to his birthplace made him the Kipling we know. Everything,

14

henceforth, tended to urge him along the path entered
on at " Westward Ho ! "

And first, the voyage in September, 1882, at the age
when the awakening soul yearns for life and drinks
in everything. Down the gloomy Thames, between
strings and clusters of great steamers from all the seas
of the world, past ghostly outlines of wharves, factories,
dockyards, giant cranes looming through the fog—
a fog in which the sickly sun turns purple, whitish, dies
out or wastes away. Then the pulse of the open sea, the
English coast, the flocks of homing ships, the long procession of lighthouses. What a revelation of England's
place in the traffic of the world ! And how some day
he will describe it all ! Standing in the bows of a great
English ship a young man whose nostrils dilate at the
first deep breath of ocean feels that he is entering
into the heritage of his race. Ushant flickers out, the
long Atlantic rollers begin to heave, the waters darken
and show a deeper blue each day. One morning the
pale, haughty spur of Gibraltar is sighted, and soon
England's proud flag again ; ironclads, forts, cannon,
casemates burrowing into the cliff on every side.
Eastward now (more British guns at Malta), from one
gate to the other of that Mediterranean, the second key
of which England already held in 1882. Then the slow
passage through the Canal (entrance and exit thereof
England's, too), and down the Red Sea (the further
issue hers again).

And from day to day the long forgotten light growing
more and more, flaming over the torpid waters, over
the torrid whiteness of the sands. Then, out of the

narrows, after the black rocks and the black coal heaps of Aden, the free spaces of the world : spaces of vaster and clearer radiance, the great levels expanding, the waters awaking under the breath of the monsoon ; magic nights and amazing dawns, when the sun leaps up, already dazzling and burning, from the fiery edge of the sea. Finally, one evening, a green strip to the east, clusters of foliage, palms, and above them the red imperial towers and domes of the poet's birthplace on the sky-line. Then perhaps he feels what one day he will write in his prelude to *The Seven Seas :* " Of no mean city am I."

As he steps on shore in the purple glare, amidst the gliding, many-coloured, bare-footed multitude, the strange Indian smell envelops him. Suddenly he knows that he has seen it all before. A half-forgotten dream takes shape again. The tide of memory rises, a strange and mighty flood, bringing back a former life, another self, dim recollections that surge one knows not whence . . . And now words, phrases of another tongue that one has ceased to understand, are on one's lips. . . .[1]

He is sixteen years and nine months old ; hardly more than a child. Impressions at that age are more definite, less mysterious than those of early childhood, but they too reach the depths and help to shape for ever a young mind. This India to which the boy has returned will take him to herself anew and work upon him.

He was not to leave her again until he was twenty-

[1] *The Tomb of his Ancestors* in *The Day's Work.*

four. The Eastern soul which had been re-born in him was to grow and take shape, but was not to be fused with the soul he had brought back from England, any more than the two languages a child learns intermingle. Such spiritual forms are comparable to two widely different ethnic types, which can be brought together but not truly combined, and so their offspring are either of the one or of the other race. In Kipling the two souls co-exist, but remain independent. He himself is well aware of this duality, and thanks the gods therefor in one of Kim's songs :

> Much I reflect on the Good and the True
> In the Faiths beneath the sun,
> But most upon Allah who gave me two
> Sides to my head, not one.

> Wesley's following, Calvin's flock,
> White or yellow or bronze,
> Shaman, Ju-ju or Angekok
> Minister, Mukamuk, Bonze—

> Here's a health, my brothers, to you,
> However your prayers are said,
> And praised be Allah who gave me two
> Separate sides to my head.

> I would go without shirt or shoe,
> Friend, tobacco or bread,
> Rather than lose for a minute the two
> Separate sides of my head !

The great difference is, however, that one side of the being is ballasted, and the other is not. Whatever may be the Oriental colour and even substance of the one, it is the other, the English side, that matters, for there lies the centre of gravity. Ten years of English discipline have given young Kipling his solid structure, his incorruptible metal. Deep down beneath all the lasting impressions he has received from India, a faith remains in him, hidden in the daily round of life, but revealed at the decisive moments ; faith in the imperative law which commands effort and devotion.

This law will be urged upon him, together with the idea of England's greatness, by all things English in this Asiatic land. First of all, by his calling. He at once became a journalist, working on the *Civil and Military Gazette* of Lahore single-handed under the editor who had engaged him on the strength of a few numbers of the *School Journal.* They had a hundred and sixty natives in the offices and printing works. He loved his profession (the smell and the noise of a composing room move him still) ; it was personal work, independence. At the age of seventeen, though living with his parents, whom he never ceased to worship (he owed all that is best in himself and his art to his father, he says), he had his own servants, his horse, his dog-cart, his club, his friends, a life of his own.[1] But in the office where he spent long nights in a temperature that for months at a time was over 100 degrees, the strain must have been great indeed. " In my own little world," he says, " the first lesson I learned was loyalty to my newspaper, and that I had to work on it in hot as in cold weather, in sickness and in health." One did not always escape fever and dysentery. . . .

[1] His father was the Director of the Lahore Museum.

RUDYARD KIPLING

To this a further lesson was added. The Anglo-Indian press of that day lived chiefly on telegrams from abroad, and fragments of articles borrowed, on a system of exchange, from the leading journals of the metropolis and of the Dominions. It was Kipling's business to receive all this material, to make cuttings, paste, summarise, and annotate. Imagine the effect on a mind trained and prepared like his, of the hours spent in this office, where the life of the entire English world enters and vibrates. News arrived in electric currents from East and West, from the two sides of the world, and it may be said that at every flash of that encounter, the consciousness of the Empire was produced in that soul.

And then travels from the Himalayas to the Deccan, first for his Lahore *Gazette*, then for the important Allahabad *Pioneer*. Success had come. He saw things, men, races, castes. His calling as a journalist, his father's name, presently the fame of his poems and his first stories, opened all doors to him; and chiefs, civil and military, feeling him to be one of themselves by birth and education, spoke their minds freely before the young man. He talked with Governors and Viceroys, with Lord Roberts himself, thus arriving at a direct, concrete idea of Government. This full experience acquired at an early age gave him from the first the true and varied matter of his stories ; and what impressed him most was, that in each of those men who represented England in India, the principle his English school had instilled into him was at work : loyalty to one's prescribed task, total and silent devotion to daily duty. The lesson he had learnt to practise at seventeen in his Lahore office all English India repeats to him, as he himself will tell us : " As to my notions of Imperialism, I learned them from men who mostly cursed their work, but always carried it through to the end, under difficult surroundings, without help or the hope of acknowledgment." Here we have almost the actual words of his *Song of the School,* that school which aimed at making men who should be masters of themselves and servants of the Empire. All Kipling's poetry reiterates this strong religion of duty. This, rather than the worship of energy, is the basis of his brilliant work.

Even in those early years the quality of that work had been recognised. Some of the tales which had appeared in his two newspapers, and then in slender volumes published at Allahabad and Bombay, are among the finest he has written. His creative power, the breadth and vigour of his vision, show themselves in these, no less than the accuracy of his line and his foreshortenings, the energy of his black and white, his skilful effects, his first-hand knowledge and his deep intuitions of souls, types, realities of all sorts. In London a few discriminating persons, and then a small section of the public, followed the swift ascent of the new planet. But about 1888 the poet was unconscious of his powers, and had not yet put forth his strength. In his *Departmental Ditties* (1886), written at odd moments, and dealing chiefly with stories of the great Anglo-Indian gossip shop—stories that go the round of regimental messes, offices, tennis courts, from the

Maidân of Calcutta to the Jokko of Simla—he was speaking to the Anglo-Indian public—not to the Empire. The earnest underlying purpose, the fervent moral, patriotic, almost religious dream which was shaping itself within him, to be expressed in his greater poems, had not yet revealed themselves.

It was his journey of 1889 which seems to have made his mission clear to him. At the age of twenty-four he left for London, where he intended to take his measure, and which he was to look at with the eyes of his own Dick Heldar returning from Upper Egypt—critical, almost foreign eyes, accustomed to dazzling light and immense spaces where life and death seem larger and simpler things.

This voyage completed his vision of the world, of the work achieved and the place held by his race therein. Eastward this time, with calls at Rangoon, Mulmein, Penang (where, in mess rooms and clubs, he hears stories of the recent Burmese War)—then at Singapore and Hong Kong, " the old rag " with its tricoloured cross greeting him in each port as in the westward journey of his childhood. He reaches Japan, where English is the second language ; he hears it on the quays of Yokohama, among the seal hunters of Frisco, Glasgow and Vancouver, who will give him the material for a startling poem. Then across the Pacific on a great Canadian liner, where his fellow-passengers are colonials, Indian officials, Scots from Manilla, Americans from California, London missionaries. In the smoking-room he hears those anecdotes which are the small change of social life among the Anglo-Saxons and postulate an Anglo-Saxon universe.

This universe he finds again in America. True, many things here astonish him: the pace of life, an apparent carelessness and disorder, souls quickly responsive to external influences, often thrilled by sudden currents of collective emotion; an alarming nervous instability, a certain cynicism of humour, a certain boastfulness, a strange bigness of conception and enterprise, a general keenness in business matters, admirable impulses of altruistic enthusiasm, and, in supreme contrast to British stiffness, curious powers of improvisation and adaptation. Nevertheless, here was but a variant of Anglo-Saxon humanity, like those which the dry climate and similar conditions of life were producing in Australia, South Africa, Canada. A new species, issuing from the old. The same tongue, the same religion, the same literature, the same ancestors. The whole germ of this civilisation had come from England: individualism and the Puritan conscience, the Bible and free competition, self-government of the community as of the individual. If the human material was beginning to change, flowing now from continental Europe, the original germ was still active, shaping the type. In this American civilisation Kipling recognised a work of his race, and there, on American soil, he conceived one of the main ideas of his poetry. This idea he defined in one of his letters to the *Pioneer*, with the high spirits of youth enjoying its freedom, and the humour of an Englishman amused by America, much as we Frenchmen of the North are by Marseilles.

RUDYARD KIPLING

But his own mission had been revealed to him when he wrote the following words :

"There must be born a poet who shall give the English the song of their own, own country—which is to say, of about half the world. Remains then only to compose the greatest song of all—The Saga of the Anglo-Saxon all round the earth—a pæan that shall combine the terrible slow swing of the *Battle Hymn of the Republic* (which, if you know not, get chanted to you) with *Britannia needs no Bulwark*, the skirl of the *British Grenadiers* with that perfect quick step, *Marching through Georgia*, and at the end, the wail of the *Dead March*. For We, even We, who share the earth between us as no gods have ever shared it, we also are mortal in the matter of our single selves. Will any one take the contract ? "

This was written in the summer of 1889. In the autumn he was in London, and from his high window on the Embankment, he looked down upon the serried infinity of little black roofs melting into the fog, like a coral shoal in the dim depths of the sea. But to the east, above the smoking wastes of brick, high phantom crosses, masts, rigging, suggest the world beyond England, distant seas and traffics. A little way along the grimy Thames rise the Gothic towers of the Houses of Parliament, bearing aloft the standard, dim and gray in the hazy sky. And behind is Westminster, the shrine of the race, where England's heroes and poets sleep, and the knightly kings of the Middle Ages, —" the Abbey that makes us say We."

There, in the ancient heart of the English world, Rudyard Kipling was in the centre whence the Empire has gradually expanded. And the following year, 1890, he had already written his *Song of the English*.

II.—THE POETRY OF IMPERIALISM

The English ; we must pause at the last word. At the time when on the other side of the Straits people were beginning to say, not *England,* but *Britain,* and when the term *British* became the official designation of the Queen's subjects, Kipling never calls them anything but *the English*. This word he uses sometimes in the widest sense, for he applies it to the *Five Nations,*[1] and even in the passage quoted above, to the dominant population of the United States; sometimes in the narrower sense which Welshmen, Irishmen and Scots especially have gradually imposed on the language by insisting that the name should not be applied to the whole, but only to one of the British peoples.

But this is pre-eminently the political nation, the one that worked in the country as its organising force, the one that gave it its power of action and expansion. The foreigner is instinctively right when he persists in speaking of the whole United Kingdom as *England*. Hence the double meaning the poet is able to give to the word. The idea is that if the Five Nations include different races, yet it was the English who founded them and built them up—that they are an English achievement, English in formation, type and culture ; that England owes her Empire to the descendant of the Angle, the Saxon, the Northman—yeoman,

[1] England, South Africa, New Zealand, Australia, Canada.

24

farmer, squire, merchant, navigator—the slow, patient, practical man, tireless in effort, indifferent to *ennui*, religious and reverent of the Law, the man whose hold on matter, virtue of silence and spontaneous discipline Carlyle has extolled—the man Defoe has shown us drawing solely upon his own inner fund of courage, endurance, activity, opposing his labour to solitude, reading the Bible and colonising, creating his *home* with his own hands, ever improving it, and because he was capable of making a law unto himself, because he was not only his own master, but master of himself, finally becoming the master of all things in his island.

Such is the type which, since Meredith and Matthew Arnold, has been contrasted on the other side of the Straits with the artistic and eloquent, fantastic and sensitive Celt, with the race that has given its most aerial and magical elements to English poetry, and has so long been pronounced unpractical (to-day it may be about to take its revenge in the domain of facts). " Celt and Saxon : " Kipling makes the same distinction as the great Welsh novelist. And it may be said that if Meredith appears as the champion of the Celt in the literature of our neighbours, Rudyard Kipling is the poet and the spokesman of the Saxon (*Saoz*, as our Bretons say).[1]

How far is this so-called Saxon type really ethnic, as generally believed, and how far is it merely a cultural product ? It is a fact that it predominates, together

[1] On the contrast between Celt and Englishman see *The Puzzler* in *Songs from Books*.

with the fair complexion, in the east of the great island, where the invaders were numerous. But it seems also that its moral qualities were progressively reinforced when under the influence of historians, novelists and moralists, they came to be considered national, opinion, education and manners being thus directed towards a new ideal of perfection. Not until the nineteenth century did the Englishman make himself so generally and so deliberately English (in the eighteenth he had aspired to be " a man of sentiment," and had loved to express his emotions).[1] Then it was that he established, at the expense of certain æsthetic and intellectual values, the worship of health and of action, the prestige of the strong man, steady-eyed, of few words, who can command because he has learnt to command himself, and is possessed by the idea of his duties. But often under the acquired impassiveness of the modern " gentleman," as under the primitive patience and stolidity of the race, deep and dangerous powers of imagination and passion lurk or slumber, and may awake suddenly to hurl a man into the fierce joys of risk, adventure and battle.

Such is the man, still Berserker at bottom, whom both Kipling and Carlyle see in the true Englishman; the ocean wanderer, the stubborn pioneer, who has carried with him everywhere English enterprise and

---

[1] Sensibility and the expression of emotion have retained their social value among the Americans, who seem to have kept certain characteristics of the English of the eighteenth century.

the English hive-instinct. He is the builder of the
Empire ! [1]

.   .   .   .   .

This Empire was at its height at the time when
Kipling revealed it. *The Seven Seas* was written
between 1890 and 1896, an interval almost corre-
sponding to that which divided Queen Victoria's two
Jubilees. The famous *Recessional*, at the end of *The
Five Nations*, ought to figure in the former series. It
belongs to 1897, the date of the apotheosis. Then,
amidst the pomp and colour of the East, the applause
of kindred nations, the thunders of the mightiest fleet
the world had ever seen gathered together, culminated
the reign, which for half a century had brought England happiness, ever-increasing wealth, territory and
prestige.

Two years later the shadows gathered, heavy from
the first with the initial defeats in the Transvaal, and
the following year the Victorian sun disappears in
this black cloud. The war is over, but doubts and
anxieties persist and become general. Are the moral,
social and political foundations of the huge English
world sound ? Has the Colossus feet of clay ? It
looks, for instance, as if the country were losing
the industrial supremacy which had given it the
markets of the world, and Joseph Chamberlain in the
course of his strenuous campaign for the economic
unity of the Empire will try to open the eyes of his
countrymen. As early as 1898 the more far-seeing

[1] On this power of inhibition in the English soul see more
especially *Et Dona Ferentes* in *The Five Nations*.

among them recognise the coming threat from Berlin
and the intended challenge to British supremacy on
the sea. A little later comes the sudden progress of
Socialism, the importation of revolutionary syndi
calism, while a spirit of criticism appears among
the new leaders of thought, attacking the manners,
prejudices, beliefs, traditions and institutions which
constitute the most English essence of England, that
organising principle, which has so long imposed on
successive generations the form and structure of the
national soul. And after these first doubts what further
almost tragic disquietudes, what disturbing visions of
discord between the existing order and the surrounding
realities were to follow !

But at the time when Kipling's success was at its
height the adaptation seemed perfect. Save in a few
lucid minds there were no misgivings. It was the
radiant end of a great age, but nothing as yet proclaimed it the end. The prestige of the Crown was
unparalleled ; the Queen was the object of an almost
religious veneration. Rites and institutions, the whole
of the ancient order was undisputed. The authority
of the Lords and Commons was unshaken and their
essence still oligarchical. The " gentleman " ruled.
In a Gladstone, a Ruskin, a Tennyson, the spiritual
greatness of the former age survived. The splendid
scarlet soldiers, erect and impassive under the old
banners of Vittoria or Ramillies, seemed the very
embodiment of strength and pride. In the statistics
of industrial production and commerce England out-
stripped all competitors. Without method or system

she steadily increased the space she occupied on the globe. Almost unwittingly Egypt, Burmah, and Zanzibar were added to her possessions.

Such was the estate, continuously and naturally growing, to which every Englishman was born and which he received as the child steps into its birthplace, in English fashion, without thinking about it. Kipling undertook to sing the glories of this estate, to reveal its greatness and its beauty to the English—*O goodly is our heritage!* he chants in the archaic diction of the Anglican liturgy—to proclaim the nobility of the title attached thereto, teaching them that these scattered possessions are a greater England exacting duties from her sons. Strange that such teaching should have been necessary and could have seemed new in a country which the foreigner looks upon as imbued with national pride (though, indeed, the word " nationalism " has no meaning save in Ireland). Patriotism is not much talked of among the English ; even in the schools nothing is said about it, perhaps because of an instinctive shrinking from big words, custom and opinion discouraging the expression of sentiment. So little is it insisted upon that the English have sometimes been thought indifferent to it and that Kipling, contrasting this reticence with the songs, speeches, ardent and spirited phrases which in the United States express the sanctity of the native land and the people's faith in the national ideal and destinies, declared in 1889 that " the average English householder seems to regard his country as an abstraction to supply him with policemen and fire brigades. The Cockney cad cannot understand what the word means . . . he would laugh in your face at the notion of any duty being owed by himself to his land."

This was playful over-statement. But perhaps among old races a man's sense of the tie that binds him to the community has become so fundamental an element of his being that it seems to disappear in daily life. It is among new nations that it tends to assert and communicate itself, as in the case of converts, thus becoming a subject for teaching and poetry. It is the Italian, the German, the American—especially the new American—who wax lyrical over their patriotism. Pent in his island for a thousand years, and having become, so to speak, a species, the Englishman is content to be English. The more profoundly English he is, the less he thinks about it. Some twenty-five years ago the people who themselves adopted the nickname of Bull were, in their habitual placidity, still " John Bull," very ignorant of the outside world, as the bull is the bull, concerned only with his own universe. They did not compare themselves with others, did not know others, which was often unpleasant to others, who took for contempt and egotism what was but insular simplicity. In those happy days these English scarcely thought of themselves as a nation amongst other nations. To rouse them to a sense of their distinct selves, opposition was needed, a shock from some competitor shutting them out from an accustomed pasture. But in face of such opposition, how strongly this consciousness arose ! How unanimously the latent patriotism sprang up in the souls of this people ! Then the *Rule Britannias*, the

RUDYARD KIPLING

By Jingos, the *Hearts of Oak*, and the *Tow-row-row* of the *British Grenadiers* rang out on every side. Such alarums became less and less frequent ; things had been settled so quickly ever since 1854. The danger in such eclipses of national feeling was, as Kipling has always seen, that in the presence of a swift, secret, and watchful enemy, the instinct of defence may awake too late, and find itself helpless in the event of sudden conflict.

As to Imperial patriotism, no one had ever thought of it in 1890. The Empire was not even a conception. And because no one had conceived it, desired it, or worked for it, it may be said that it did not exist, save in India, where Disraeli had proclaimed the old Queen *Kaisar-i-Hind* like the Moguls, in order to naturalise the Sovereign and increase her prestige. There was an Indian Empire, but of a British Empire no one spoke. Not only did the word correspond to nothing organic or really organised (and this is still the case), but it stood for no moral reality, for no collective whole linked together by a spiritual bond. There was Great Britain with her colonies ; some of these were great countries no less self-governing than England herself. The term *Dominions* was adopted in 1907, to avoid any suggestion of tutelage or vassalage. Between these nations and the Mother Country the sentimental tie was so weak that each seemed destined to follow where America had led. Separation was the logical conclusion which every one had foretold when Canada was given Home Rule at the beginning of Queen Victoria's reign. Indeed, that country had already threatened to ally itself with the United States, and

Australia had set up immigration barriers which in fact excluded the British workman as well as the yellow races. From the competition of the old country the Dominions protected themselves by tariffs. Such was the indifference of each dependency about the year 1886 that Mr. Chamberlain predicted : If ever England should be involved in a war, the colonies would drift away and finally detach themselves altogether.

These prophecies caused no consternation. England had swarmed, and each swarm having made its hive on the pattern of the mother hive, was growing and living its own independent life more and more. It was believed and constantly repeated, that it was because the English had never premeditated anything, never organised anything systematically, because they had expanded by natural methods, by the activity of the individual, bearing in himself the hive principle, together with the experience, custom and instinct of the species, that they held such a great place in the world.[1]

Family feeling, too, is a thing of nature, but it requires to be kept up. It is not very strong in Anglo-Saxon countries, where men are primarily alive to the practical and the immediate, where the nearest of kin part easily to seek their fortunes afar, and then forget each other. English they remain in type and civilisation, but the new environment absorbs them rapidly,

[1] " Nowhere is the distrust of what is termed ' logic ' so firmly rooted as in England ; a course of conduct which stands out as sharply ' logical ' is in itself suspect."—J. A. HOBSON, *Imperialism*, p. 221.

and before long they call themselves, not Englishmen, but Australians or Canadians. A curious trait in these people, in whom what we now call race shows itself in characteristics so pronounced and so obvious, is the weakness of the race idea, nowadays so active in the rest of the world, unless it be brought home to them by the presence of coloured populations or of a civilisation sharply opposed to their own. The English mind is not much influenced by abstract ideas, and where it is dominant we shall not find the State intent on their propagation.

Three years before the Boer War, the shock of which was to stir all the English nations, and unify them morally, and nearly twenty years before the Great War, Kipling did them a signal service when, in *The Seven Seas*, he celebrated their common blood and common memories, thus preparing the movement towards reunion. In these poems (most of which were written earlier, but then collected for the first time), the theme of Empire was first sounded. Let us understand clearly what was meant by the term; it tends to create a wrong impression, and therefore attempts to substitute for it the word *Commonwealth* have often been made. The Empire is the comity of English nations; Imperialism is the consciousness of Empire. The word, Lord Milner has told us, has a moral significance.[1] Of course, in England as else-

[1] " It is a mistake to think of Imperialism as principally concerned with extension of territory, with ' painting the map red.' It is a question of preserving the unity of a great race."—LORD MILNER, *The Nation and the Empire.*

where, there have always been men and parties who have dreamt of painting all the map red. But Kipling's idea is quite clear ; the Empire in his poetry stands for defence, not conquest—soon for defence against an Imperialism of a very different stamp. He proclaims, not the supremacy, but the brotherhood of the English throughout the world. He urges them to recognise one another, to lay the spiritual foundations of the British United States, to revive and uphold the family name and feeling across the seas, to perpetuate the alliance of brothers. Remember that he called himself " the singer of a clan."

* * *

In Germany the dream of Empire and the thirst for conquest were inspired by dissertations on history and philosophy, by professorial disquisitions. In England souls had to be stirred by images, a poetry at once realistic and lyrical ; poetry of an essentially concrete quality in which, quickened by living, stirring pulsations, rhythms, sounds, colours, impulses, aspirations mingle together, expressing with the most significant moods of things the most intense states of the inner being. The great aspects of the English world as developed by the English soul—that soul itself with its deeply rooted characteristics and its peculiar reactions— such was the theme of the poet of the *Seven Seas*.

He sang, above all, the epic of the English and the sea, the field of their adventure—their yearning for adventure and for the sea. In verses that breathe a desire rising from atavic depths, he evokes from one pole to the other the great waters of the globe, the true domain of his race and its appointed portion : *the Ocean at large, our share*. And this he does with rhythms now slow and inevitable as the rise and swell of rollers, now full of the tumult and fury of the storm (*the yelling Channel tempest when the siren hoots and roars*), now suggesting a placidity immense as the slumber of the element itself. Waters of the North, white between the floes, veiled by curtains of snow, waters vanishing under their own mists, gray bare waters stealing between the granite rocks and noiselessly lifting the languid fronds of sea-wrack. Then the *lineless level floors* in the long summer evenings, the free Atlantic and its oily swell before a storm, the dazzled torpor of the Line, and the blue monotony of the southern seas, where the great sailing ships keep on the same tack for weeks, under the white clouds steadily driven along by the Trades. And together with the sea, the things of the sea and of sailors, the lighthouses with " weed about their knees," their " loins battered by the swing-ing, smoking seas " ; and in the silence and darkness of the abyss, the cables, quivering with tremors that are the thoughts of men. And then the vessels, " swift shuttles of an Empire's loom," from the schooner which weighs anchor in port, and trembling, feels her way in the night, yearning for wind and water and space, to the great mail steamer which three weeks ago was wrestling with the fogs and foul weather of the dark " fiftieth north," and now nearing the splendid girdle of the world sees strange coasts glide past like scenes from fairyland—from the rough collier, black with smoke and soot, to the aristocratic liner, to the six thousand horse-power destroyer, low and gray in the gray surf under the rainy sky of five o'clock, bringing swift death to her chosen prey. He has not even forgotten the derelict, soulless now since man has left her—bleached by salt and sun, rolling and swinging at the mercy of tides and waves, " blind in the hot blue ring," and turning, drifting under stars which " mock the prow that cannot hold one true."

The sea is magnetic—the free expanse over which dream and yearning reach out towards the unknown. In how many English souls, from the Vikings and the Saxon sea rovers to the city clerk and the shopman pining for air and space beneath the factory roofs and the smoke of modern England, has that aspiration stirred ? The singer tells of the dream that may haunt man in *the man-stifled town*. He himself has felt the passion for the Beyond, the call of the horizon where the masts of the ships go down ; his Tramp-Royal has described

How something in my 'ead upset me all,
Till I 'ad dropped whatever 'twas for good,
An' out at sea be'eld the dock lights die,
An' met my mate—the wind that tramps the world.

And so, with pulsing rhythms that translate their fevers and their vehemence, he can praise the adventurers of the seas, the discoverers of new lands, the pioneers in those lands, true founders of the Empire, all those who showed the way, because to them *came the Whisper, came the Vision, came the Power with the Need*—the men whose skeletons are rotting on the sea floors, and those who went before them to the icebergs of the Pole, to the veldt and the prairie, and were struck down by hunger and thirst and cold. Following the trail marked by their bones, the English entered into their heritage.[1]

And above all, the Empire, the completed Empire, the Colonies, the Dominions, each marshalled in its turn, with its light, its landscapes, its peculiar, memory-laden scents. The breathless mornings of the austral world, the haze of the smouldering bush fires, the far-flung, fenceless prairie, where the quick cloud shadows trail, the plough in the league-long furrow, followed by the gulls from the Great Lakes ; floods and thunders, and then the pale dry blue of South Africa, and the smell of the blazing Karroo ; the dear dark foster-mothers of India and their heathen songs ; the cool of the deep verandahs, the blaze of the jewelled main, the palms in the moonlight, the fire-flies among the canes.[2] In *The Song of the English*, when the dead have spoken, bearing witness to the laying down of their lives, when the sons have vowed to serve, all the great cities of the Empire stand forth and proclaim themselves : Bombay, noisy with the roar of a thousand factories, with the babel of all nations in her bazaars ; Calcutta, born from the river mud—" death in her hands, but gold " ; Madras, whom Clive had kissed on mouth and eyes, once crowned above all other queens, still dreaming of her ancient glory ; Victoria, where West changes to East, the well-forged link in the tested chain of Empire, and all the others, rising in turn and making

---

[1] *Song of the Dead.*
[2] *The Native-Born, passim.*

obeisance to the old mother, gray-haired England, who greets her children and replies :

Truly ye come of The Blood ; slower to bless than to ban ;
Little used to lie down at the bidding of any man.
Flesh of the flesh that I bred, bone of the bone that I
    bare ;
Stark as your sons shall be—stern as your fathers were.
Deeper our speech than love, stronger than life our
    tether,
But we do not fall on the neck nor kiss when we come
    together.
My arm is nothing weak, my strength is not gone by,
Sons, I have borne many sons, but my dugs are not dry.
Look, I have made you a place and opened wide the
    doors,
That ye may talk together, your Barons and
    Councillors—
Wards of the Outer March, Lords of the Lower Seas,
Ay, talk to your gray mother that bore you on her knees !
That ye may talk together, brother to brother's face—
Thus for the good of your peoples—thus for the pride of
    the Race.
Also, we will make promise. So long as the Blood
    endures,
I shall know that your good is mine ; ye shall feel that
    my strength is yours,
In the day of Armageddon, at the last great fight of all,
That our House stand together and the pillars do not
    fall.[1]

These lines were written in 1890. They belong to the first poem in *The Seven Seas*, published in 1896. A few years later was fought the Boer War—not the

---

[1] *Armageddon*, the apocalyptic name given to the Great War by the English as early as August, 1914. See Revelation xvi. 16.

RUDYARD KIPLING

Great War, the Armageddon foretold in *The Song of the English*—yet it revealed the collective soul of the Empire, and in the emotion that stirred them all the Five Nations acknowledged their sisterhood. Immediately after the crisis Kipling published *The Five Nations*.

Here the earlier work, continued from 1897 to 1903, is gradually expanded and adapted to the new facts which set new questions of life and death to the English world. At first nothing is changed : the Victorian reign is still calm and fair ; it culminates with the second Jubilee and still continues. The poet dwells on the same themes : the sea, the ships, the soldiers, the emigrants and explorers, the longing for distant horizons, the patient struggle against desert, plague, inundation, the unfaltering effort of the English in the old, decrepit East to establish order, education and justice, their devotion to the white man's tasks.[1]

But with the crisis in the Transvaal the point of view changes, and other watchwords must be accepted. The spiritual union of the English peoples is accomplished, needless now to quicken the sense of it by extolling the Empire. The stirring music that was to awaken pride of race is stilled. It is a notable trait in the so-called Imperialist poet, that the war provoked him to no martial gesture, no word of hatred or defiance to the enemy. Of the sturdy, patient adversary [2] he speaks gravely and respectfully—of the devastation

---

[1] *Pharaoh and the Serjeant* (1897) ; *Kitchener's School* (1898).

[2] *General Joubert* (1900).

as an organised madness, a bloody dream, after which the former foes must clasp hands, and " repair the wrong that was done to the living and the dead." Together let them fight against their common enemies : hail, frost, flood, " the red and rustling cloud that blows the locusts' mile-deep swarm "; together let them wage the " holy wars that have no truce 'twixt seed and harvest time," till the young corn covers the evil dream of hate.[1]

And when it is a question of England, his attitude is the reverse of Imperialistic pride. No longer need he sing *The Song of the English ;* the united English must be prepared now for the perils of another war and to this end must be told of the weaknesses which are their sins ; they must be alarmed and forced to search into their own consciences. Here the " tribal singer " begins to show himself a prophet, a prophet like those of ancient Israel, and above all, a judge, the judge of his people who have forgotten the Law, speaking to them unsparingly, turning them back to the eternal truths. In vehement and direct words, he addresses them with the stark, authoritative vigour which the English brought up on the Bible associate with the idea of absolute right and religion. Certain of these poems are scourgings, such as those Isaiah inflicted on the erring tribes. In our days no country but England (perhaps because she is so strong and so sure of herself) would allow her sons to use language so free and daring. Carlyle and Ruskin, who were also prophets, and recognised as such, had already

[1] *The Settler* (1902).

chastised their countrymen with similar scorpions. But the operation had seemed less premeditated. · Here the whip was applied deliberately, in scientific and almost cruel fashion, calculated to make a durable impression on a tough skin. What more scathing satire could be written on the English, asleep in their ancient habits and prejudices, their traditional well-being and illusion of security, than the poem called *The Old Men?*

Because we know we have breath in our mouth and
    think we have thought in our head,
We shall assume that we are alive, whereas we are
    really dead.
We shall not acknowledge that old stars fade, or alien
    planets arise,
Or any new compass wherewith new men adventure
    'neath new skies.
We shall lift up the ropes that constrained our youth to
    bind on our children's hands ;
We shall call to the water below the bridges to return
    and replenish our lands ;
We shall harness horses (Death's own pale horses), and
    scholarly plough the sands.
We shall lie down in the eye of the sun for lack of a
    light on our way—
We shall rise up when the day is done, and chirrup,
    " Behold it is day ! "
We shall abide till the battle is won ere we amble into
    the fray.

How near these words were one day to come to a tragic fulfilment ! Here, translated into the vehement language of the poet, but more definite and menacing, is the warning that the future King George V., returning from his travels through the Empire and his review of his people, was to give to the English of the island : *Wake up, England !* Kipling was of the Empire. He had always looked at the Islanders with eyes very different from their own. He had sung their virtues—yet how clearly he saw their faults, which are but those very virtues when they no longer answer to necessities !—their slowness, which we admire when manifested as patience ; their slavery to habit, which may also be called respect for tradition ; their lack of adaptability, so closely akin to their power of resistance; their self-sufficiency, which may reveal itself as insufficiency, yet is their certitude and their pride. His mission it was to move that England, which disdains emotion, to shake the " bull-nation," to open its eyes forcibly, and as he had already undertaken to do more than once (he had acknowledged the difficulty of the task, but he was a master of the art), " to make the Britisher sit up." It was essential to drive home to this people, to make them digest and assimilate " the phenomenal lesson " which the Boer farmers had given them, not " under the trees, nor yet in the shade of a tent, but swingingly, over eleven degrees of a bare brown continent, with a fulness accorded to no other land " ; the " imperial lesson," the effects of which would be felt not in " our mere astonied camps, but in Council and Creed and College, and all the obese, unchallenged old things that stifle and overlie us."[1]

This lesson, which *The Old Men* had set forth in general terms, was uttered more pitilessly, precisely

[1] *The Lesson* (1902).

and completely in *The Islanders*, and here we have not
only the accent, but often the abrupt utterance and the
actual vocabulary of the Bible :

*No doubt but ye are the People—your throne is above the
    King's.*
*Whoso speaks in your presence must say acceptable
    things :*
Bowing the head in worship, bending the knee in fear—
*Bringing the word well smoothen—such as a King should
    hear.*

Fenced by your careful fathers, ringed by your leaden
    seas,
Long did ye wake in quiet and long lie down at ease ;
Till ye said of Strife, " What is it ? " of the Sword, " It
    is far from our ken " ;
Till ye made a toy of your shrunken hosts and a toy of
    your armed men.

Ye stopped your ears to the warning—ye would neither
    look nor heed—
Ye set your leisure before their toil and your lusts above
    their need.
Because of your witless learning and your beasts of
    warren and chase,
Ye grudged your sons to their service and your fields for
    their camping-place.

Ye forced them to glean in the highways the straw for
    the bricks they brought ;
Ye forced them to follow in byways the craft that ye
    never taught.
Ye hindered and hampered and crippled ; ye thrust out
    of sight and away
Those that would serve you for honour and those that
    would serve you for pay.

Then were the judgments loosened; then was your
    shame revealed,
At the hands of a little people, few but apt in the field.
Yet ye were saved by a remnant (and your land's long-
    suffering Star),
When your strong men cheered in their millions while
    your striplings went to the war.

Sons of the sheltered city—unmade, unhandled,
    unmeet—
Ye pushed them raw to the battle as ye picked them raw
    from the street.
And what did ye look they should compass? Warcraft
    learned in a breath,
Knowledge unto occasion at the first far view of death?

So! And ye train your horses and the dogs ye feed and
    prize?
How are the beasts more worthy than the souls you
    sacrifice?
But ye said, " Their valour shall show them "; but ye
    said, " The end is close."
And ye sent them comfits and pictures to help them
    harry your foes,

And ye vaunted your fathomless power, and ye
    flaunted your iron pride,
Ere—ye fawned on the Younger Nations for the men
    who could shoot and ride!
Then ye returned to your trinkets; then ye contented
    your souls
With the flannelled fools at the wicket or the muddied
    oafs at the goals.

This final shaft stung the most. I remember the
sensation, almost the scandal created, when in 1902
the *Times* published *The Islanders*. (It was then the

practice of that newspaper to print these solemn appeals
of the poet to the nation on its front page.) For the
first time an Englishman spoke contemptuously of
those English games which are looked upon as a
national discipline, and which in the nineteenth century
were almost as potent a factor as the Bible in the
formation of English character.[1] Had not Wellington
said that Waterloo was won on the playing fields of
Eton, and had not Kipling himself four years earlier
instanced these very games as one of the secrets, so
unintelligible to subject races, of English supremacy?[2]
Yes, but meanwhile there had been that imperial, that
phenomenal lesson, " very cheap at the price," and it
remained for those who had paid for it to profit by it.
In the recent crisis the English house had shown itself
more time-worn than its owners had thought. Against
a much greater peril, already threatening in 1902, it
would not suffice to strengthen the building. It
would be necessary to go down to the foundations,
to question principles hitherto accepted as indisputable,
such, for instance, as the sacrosanct " liberty of
the subject," which was, in all minds, fundamentally
opposed to conscription. A difficult enterprise, in
a country where this principle is an ancient subject
for pride, where the pressure of habit is so great,
where, above all, no class is specially interested in the
question, no party disposed to risk its popularity on

[1] Of course Kipling's attack was chiefly aimed at the
spectacular games played by professionals, which attract
a mob of loafers and betting men.

[2] *Kitchener's School* (1898) in *The Five Nations*.

the issue. Twelve years later something more than a threat was needed to bring about the reform : imminent peril. In 1902, Kipling's idea fell on dry ground ; nevertheless, it was a germ, and the rough strokes of his pickaxe prepared the soil.

He alone could have uttered such words. There was indeed a poet laureate, the official successor of Tennyson ; but the national poet, recognised as such since his religious poem on the Jubilee, was Kipling. And this he was, not only because more forcibly than all others he had conceived and expressed the idea of race, country and Empire, but because no other had so completely rendered the elementary and essential characteristics of the English soul. Tennyson had seized certain traits, and his *Ode on the Death of the Duke of Wellington*, singing, not the hero's glory, but his silent devotion to duty, had excited a current of emotion almost comparable to the effect of the *Recessional*. But his refined and literary art, full of classic and Celtic echoes, strong as was its appeal to the cultured classes, could not reach the deeper strata of the country. On the other hand, many of Kipling's poems went to the hearts of soldiers and sailors, clerks and shopmen, settlers of the Veldt and the Far West. Not that all his work springs from primitive depths. Many of his inventions are conscious poetry, sometimes complex and abstruse, verging on prose, even on obscure prose. But when his idea is spontaneous, it is clear enough, and expressed in rhythm of unprecedented vigour. Then its influence is far-reaching, because, in essence, expression and movement, it harmonises with the deepest and most general tendencies of a world-wide public. Let us now see from what strength of soul, what powers of vision and faith its magic is derived.

III.—THE POETRY OF ENERGY

The quality which gives these poems of the first period their essentially English character is a certain fulness and tension of spiritual energy—that energy of life and character which the national training of body and soul, together with the general system of social discipline, seek to guard and develop in a particular class of English society.

This it is which makes Kipling's poetry so healthy, strangely unlike the disquieting music, full of doubt and unrest, which we have learnt from famous models to accept as the characteristic of the poet. It is instinct with action and will, with tonic movements ranging from outbursts of joyous invention to sustained accents of enthusiasm and solemn conviction. A man's voice was heard in these first poems of Kipling's. It compelled attention at once. No tone could have been more sharply opposed to those vague moods of longing, foreboding, contemplation, ecstasy, the unutterable essence of which the Pre-Raphaelites—Rossetti, Burne-Jones and others—had tried to convey. Kipling's verses are like the strokes of a hammer wielded by the brawny arms of a blacksmith. The character thus revealed was at once recognised by the first readers of *The Light that Failed*. They had guessed how much of himself and his poetry Kipling, at the age of twenty-six, had put into the person and the work of his Dick Heldar : the sudden fits of dreaming, the wild desire, the elemental energy which concentrates and battles, sensibility to the simplest and most intense aspects of nature and of man, swift and penetrating vision, and in the recoil of the mind upon itself, the sudden development of the conception born of the image received. Painter and poet, the soul was the same in both. And, indeed, the painter is so much a poet that his intensity is revealed to us by the fever into which he is thrown by some lines he hears recited one evening.

I remember the day when I first read the fragments of verse that occur in the novel. Some one was playing the piano, and the musician, passing from one thing to another, began a piece of Schumann's, which ought, I know, to have snatched me away from any book. I did not even hear it ; the beat of the English metre was so strong and imperious that it seemed to silence the subtle, tender music of the composer of *The Jasmine*. All the most characteristic pieces of this poet have this quality. The movement of the soul from which they spring seems to upheave the surface of the verse, gathering force in its progress like the periodic wave of a ground swell. Nothing could be newer or more varied than his metres, yet they never suggest research. The rhythm seems the result of a natural force. It has that indefinable touch of the elemental and inevitable which also marks the idea, its presentation, the marshalling of the details, the culminating effect—

RUDYARD KIPLING

marks in fact the whole of a Kipling story or poem ; and hence that saying, in the early days, that his art could no more be discussed than a cannon ball hitting one in the chest. No French translation can express such energy of rhythm. This is possible only in English, thanks to the intensity of the tonic accent, gaining strength under the stress of emotion, which inflects and modulates speech after the manner of music (hence the frequent use of italics in English writing to mark this special emphasis of the phrase). And this goes so far in some cases that the verbal music is almost enough, the meaning of the words becoming a secondary matter. Such is the case, for instance, in *The Anchor Song*, with its technical vocabulary, which, when translated into French, is but a long conundrum for the landsman. With the English version, no matter if the reader be ignorant of the nautical terms, the amazing palpitation of the metre acts upon him, and in the rush and racket of the verses he is conscious at once of straining arms hauling at the sheets, flapping sails, tumult of wind and water—of the desire and then the rapture of the open sea.

The same energy, the same movements, expressed by Kipling's rhythms, are evident in all his art. On a former occasion, when dealing with his tales, we tried to define his vision and his style. In this respect there is no difference at all between the poet and the prose writer. In both there is the same thrust of the sensation, the same energetic reaction seizing on the truest and most concentrated expression, on the most pregnant and moving image ; in both there is the same concision, and consequently the same lyric value conferred on accurate and realistic words, the same spontaneity, the same certitude, the same stark abruptness of expression, the same unexpected and almost startling effects. But in the poems we feel the influence of the Bible, the old book which is also the expression of a fervid soul. To this influence the art of all great English writers since the Reformation has been subjected, through the superb sixteenth century version. Add to this the power peculiar to the English language, the language of poetry above all others, because in it the word is so near to the image, because there is one for every movement of the soul, for every shade and degree of the object and the sensation. And in Kipling's verse the vocabulary is most intensely English, rich in monosyllabic words and clanking alliterations, like those of the violent Anglo-Saxon poems.

By this quality of force the artist's sympathies are governed. His spirit is attuned to the tonic aspect of things, to those which express great, simple energies. If we wished to define him by a contrast, we should oppose to him Shelley, the poet of the fainting ecstatic soul, of the Sensitive Plant, of perfumes, the poet who shows matter only in its radiant, or, as spiritualists would say, its astral state. No lyric poet has sung so little of flowers and moonlight, so rarely written the word : love. But how he has looked at the world, how well he knows the sea, the greatest visible energy in our world—the sea and all the things thereof ! How he reproduces its life and movement in himself, and passes them on to us ! The pallid, foaming fury

of the storm, the wild clamour on the reef or sand-
bank of the bell-buoy, plunging, tossing, quivering
in the choppy tide when the wind blows against the
galloping rush of the ebb : " By the gates of Doom
I sing, On the horns of Death I ride." And then
" the sleek-barrelled swell before storm, gray, formless,
enormous and growing ; " or " the heave and the halt
and the hurl and the crash of the comber wind-
hounded ; " and again in the darkness : " the shudder,
the stumble, the swerve as the star-stabbing bowsprit
emerges." Finally :

The orderly clouds of the Trades, and the ridged roaring
sapphire thereunder. . . .[1]

The English verse with its suggestion of immensity
is untranslatable. If among Kipling's readers—they
are everywhere—there is one who from a topmast has
looked out, towards noon, across the dazzling circle of
the tropical waters, here he will find his vision again.
But any one who knows English feels the suggestions
of such a rhythm, which recalls the English translation
of the Psalms—feels the power of the long, sustained
syllables, the vague protracted rustle of the alliteration,
like the muffled thunder rising from the whole sea ; and
finally the majesty of the last word, prolonging the
cadence, and also suggesting the grand tonalities of the
Bible. For here strength rises to the level of majesty,
and the solemn emotion of the soul as it contemplates
the waste of planetary waters, bare and open to the
sun, partakes of religion.

[1] *The Sea and the Hills* in *The Five Nations.*

ENGLISH LITERATURE

In the poet's vision of humanity, the same tendency is apparent. There, again, it is to power that he is most susceptible, to those states and aspects of man which denote the plenitude and freshness of vital energies, the force of the active will resisting, fighting, or expanding in triumph. One of his finest songs is the great triumphal chant of Mowgli over the corpse of his enemy, Shere Khan, the rhythmic repetitions of which (we seem to hear the trampling of the feet), the sudden movements, the cries of exultation and defiance, recall the wild grandeur of the Song of Deborah.

But Mowgli is a Hindu, capable of the alternations of violence and languor which characterise the frenzied rhapsodists of the East. In Kipling's poetic work, the East plays no such important part as in his tales. It is English energy that the poet of the English, evoking the men, things and powers of the Empire, primarily sings and serves. Of this energy the most salient feature is its stability ; but its forms vary. At the higher degree of tension it attains to the loftiest spirituality ; and of all its moods, it is this which interests the poet more and more. But it has also its elemental states, in which it still partakes copiously of Nature and matter. This, it would seem, is what he loved so much in the " soldiers of the Queen," the sturdy, well-set-up troops of the old English Regular Army, whom he gazed on in his youth with the same passionate attention as the unhappy hero of *The Light that Failed.*

From 1890 to 1892 this army gave him the matter

for one of his first collections of verse, the *Barrack Room Ballads*, which were to achieve popularity among soldiers, and the movement and style of which recall those of the songs sold at the doors of East End " pubs." Of these refrains, the beat of which is like the tramp of a battalion on the march, the hero is Tommy Atkins, as he used to be seen in the streets of London—his chest thrown out under the scarlet tunic, his cane in his hand, his cap at the regulation angle, the strap across his chin—rhythmically swinging his magnificent person, swaggering, and laying siege to barmaids ; or else, under African or Asiatic skies, khaki-clad, helmet on head, toiling and sweating behind camels, elephants and mules. And, with him, we have his beer, his shilling a day, his cricket, his embarkation on troopships, his confused vision of foreign lands, where the natives call him *Sahib*, of naked multitudes swarming on the red soil at the feet of monstrous idols. And then the picturesque and strong vulgarity of his speech, with its " bloodys " and " bloomings " ; and also his inherent honesty, his faith in good food and smart bearing, his vague yet potent idea of the Queen and the Empire (" Walk wide o' the Widow at Windsor "), his home-sick dreaming, at night, to the music of the banjo, his simple and sombre fatalism when the breath of cholera pursues the regiment under the warm rains, his grave and obscure sense of the solemn and religious when he says : " O my Gawd ! "—his whole soul in short, and his whole life, from the angry moods and the freaks of the young soldier in the making who kicks over the traces, to the fine, healthy adaptation of the true professional; from his first, tense anguish when, with set teeth, he faces the enemy's fire—

" And now the hugly bullets come pecking through the
    dust,
  And no one wants to face them, but every beggar
    must. . . ."

to the experience and the finished type of the old sergeant-shepherd, who holds his men in hand under fire, and finally sweeps them forward to the attack :

'E's just as sick as they are, and 'is 'eart is like to split,
But 'e works 'em, works 'em, works 'em, till 'e feels 'em
    take the bit ;
The rest is 'oldin' steady till the watchful bugles play,
An' 'e lifts 'em, lifts 'em, lifts 'em through the charge
    that wins the day.

These ballads were really addressed to soldiers. They were sung in the barracks and camps of India, at the hour when the men light their pipes and turn to the bard of the regiment, who was able to mingle them with his usual refrains. The vocabulary, the style, the movements, the highly coloured pathos, the obvious moral, were those of artless popular pictures.

But here we feel the hand of a great artist. For these rough traits are full of a general sense, show-ing the fundamentals of a race—in the first place what may be called a certain stolidity of the mind, which keeps it in a given groove, and makes for reticence, greater mobility being essential to the southern play of speech, with its swift banter and lively, lucid ideas. And then a certain subjective intensity shown in the man's powers of resistance, tenacity, self-absorption and accumulated passion. On such souls impressions are rarely made, but then they are lasting. Slowly but deeply moved souls, these, in which a sudden shock may rouse latent forces of imagination, strange, vivid dreaming, rising sometimes to solemn mystic visions. Hence the success of the Salvation Army and of its methods, so alien to us, and ineffectual in Latin countries. Hence the many conversions, the drama of which sometimes suddenly reveals itself, but more often remains hidden and continues to grow inwardly.

Thus in the poem called *Mulholland's Contract* we are told of a sailor in charge of the lower deck of a cattle boat. One stormy night the lights go out, and the pens break up one by one, rolling the animals in confusion. Terror-struck, the man makes a compact with God. He is saved by a miracle, escaping with a wound on his head; and during his convalescence in the Seaman's Hospital, where his chief occupation is to read " the shiny Scripture texts " on the wall, God speaks to him. The voice tells him to go back to the cattle boats, the most dangerous of all sea-faring craft, where men's souls are nearer Hell than anywhere else, and to preach to the ungodly, the blasphemers, the fornicators, so numerous among the sea-dogs.[1]

More complete is the typically vigorous portrait of old Sir Anthony Gloster, the sometime merchant service skipper, then the creator and principal shareholder of a line of trading vessels, now one of the magnates of the mercantile marine. He is no saint; he has, indeed, certain rascalities on his conscience, which do

[1] *Mulholland's Contract* (1894).

not seem to weigh him down unduly. In his young days he had been commissioned by a shady company to take crazy old vessels to sea and founder them, for the sake of the insurance. Later on, he defrauded his partner's heirs by appropriating some designs for a patent which he found among the dead man's papers. Everything he touched has succeeded ; his life has been all audacity, enterprise, struggle, lust of power and domination. The most vulgar, the most combative, the most arrogant of parvenus. Now he is on his death-bed and he speaks to his son, of whom he has made a gentleman (" Harrer an' Trinity College ! " . . . " I stood you an education. . . .")—the son he despises as a drawing-room puppet, a dilettante, a good-for-nothing who has not even been able to give him a grandson. He talks in his loose, brutal fashion, with words that show his lifelong craving for authority—a long monologue interspersed with Biblical reminiscences and sacred phrases, and illuminated by abrupt, soul-stirring visions, that have in them something of the nature of great poetry. He knows that he is about to die : " Never seen death yet, Dickie ? . . . Well, now is your time to learn ! " But the images of the past rise up before him, and among them there is one which recurs, a culminating image, symbolising the glory of success. Each time it comes up his voice rises, and his dying hand is clenched in supreme exultation of pride and triumph : " Ten thousand men on the pay-roll and forty freighters at sea ! "

He reviews his beginnings, the old tubs he sailed when he was twenty-three, his marriage at twenty-four,

his first venture : " half shares in a cheap un . . .
patching and coaling on credit " ; his swift success, his
growing enterprises : the foundry, the forges, the sheds,
the workshops for engine-building ; and in those early
days of steam navigation, the march he stole on his
rivals, still " piffling with iron " when he had given his
orders for steel ! " Steel and the first expansions."
Not in vain had he learnt at school the Scripture text :
" Let your light shine a little in front of the next ! "
And then the six-inch rollers, which paid him sixty per
cent., the invention he had found among his late
partner's papers : " I'm no fool to finish if a man will
give me a hint (I remember his widow was angry). . . ."

And together with these professional reminiscences
his gibes at his son, memories of his mistresses, and
then deeper and more solemn thoughts of his dead
wife, the wife who died long ago, and came back one
night to warn him against drink. She had gone with
him on his long sea-trips, had made a man of him,
urging him to aim at something higher than a skipper's
berth on a merchant vessel. She had given him a
child on each voyage ; but, born at sea, " they died,
poor little beggars ! Only you, an' you stood it ; you
'aven't stood much beside ! . . . We dropped her—I
think I told you—and I pricked it off where she sank—

[Tiny she looked on the grating—that oily, treacly
    sea—].

Hundred and eighteen East, remember, and South,
    just three."

For these are his instructions, his last wishes : he
means to join her, to go to the Little Paternosters,

south of Macassar, in the *Mary Gloster*, one of his own steamers, the vessel on which she died thirty years before, and there they are to drop him overboard, just where she sank. There are five thousand pounds waiting for his son if his orders are duly carried out. M'Andrew, the old chief engineer, knows what is to be done.

" He'll take the *Mary* in ballast—you'll find her a lively
    ship ;
And you'll take Sir Anthony Gloster, that goes on 'is
    wedding trip,
Lashed in our old deck-cabin with all three portholes
    wide,
The kick of the screw beneath him, and the round blue
    seas outside.
Sir Anthony Gloster's carriage—our 'ouse-flag flying
    free—
Ten thousand men on the pay-roll and forty freighters
    at sea.
He made himself and a million, but this world is a
    fleeting show,
And he'll go to the wife of 'is bosom the same as he
    ought to go—
By the heel of the Paternosters—there isn't a chance to
    mistake—
And Mac'll pay you the money as soon as the bubbles
    break.
Five thousand for six weeks' cruising, the stanchest
    freighter afloat,
And Mac he'll give you your bonus the minute I'm out
    of the boat.
He'll take you round to Macassar, and you'll come back
    alone ;
He knows what I want o' the *Mary* . . . I'll do what
    I please with my own."

What he wants, what he has thought out—he says enough to enable us to guess—is a monstrous act, an act of destruction devised by pride and by an imagination the gloomy grandeur of which links this coarse modern parvenu with certain violent poets of his race. M'Andrew is to come back and sink the ship where his body was sunk.

> "... I'll do what I please with my own.
> Your mother 'ud call it wasteful, but I've seven and
>   thirty more ;
> I'll come in my private carriage and bid it wait at the
>   door."

And gradually the sentimental, moralising, religious dream comes back, flooding the soul of this old freebooter, and this dream again is one of the underlying elements of the English soul.

> "Flesh of my flesh, my dearie, for ever an' ever,
>   Amen !—
> That first stroke come for a warning ; I ought to ha'
>   gone to you then.
> Mary, why didn't *you* warn me ? I've allus heeded
>   to you,
> Excep'—I know—about women ; but you are a spirit
>   now ;
> An' wife, they was only women, and I was a man.
>   That's how.
> An' a man 'e must go with a woman, as you could not
>   understand ;
> But I never talked 'em secrets. I paid 'em out o' hand.
> Thank Gawd, I can pay for my fancies : Now what's
>   five thousand to me
> For a berth off the Paternosters in the haven where I
>   would be ? [1]

[1] Psalm cvii. 30.

I believe in the Resurrection, if I read my Bible plain.
But I wouldn't trust 'em at Woking ; we're safer at sea
    again.
For the heart it shall go with the treasure, go down to
    the sea in ships.[1]
I'm sick of the hired women—I'll kiss my girl on her
    lips.
I'll be content with my fountain, I'll drink from my
    own well,
And the wife of my youth shall charm me [2]—an' the
    rest can go to Hell."

The monologue finishes strangely. The man is about
to die ; he feels the apoplectic rush of blood in his
brain and his own physical agitation becomes confused
with his dream, with the vision of his sinking ship—
sinking " by the head." This sudden flood which he
feels rising is the water invading the empty hold,
" churning an' choking an' chuckling, quiet an' scummy
an' dark, full to her lower hatches and risin'
steady. . . ." Suddenly there is a commotion, a dull
shock ; the after bulkhead gives way, and " flooded
from stem to stern " the ship begins to settle down.

English words alone can render not only this essentially English vision of things, but moods and shades of
feeling peculiar to a certain English caste. In what
other tongue would such a mixture of nautical and
Biblical terms, slang and the most majestic of all
styles be possible ? And where but in an Anglo-Saxon
country could the same soul combine traits to our
minds so irreconcilable ? Realism and mysticism,

---

[1] Matthew vi. 21, and Psalm cvii. 23.
[2] Proverbs v. 15.

sentiment and brutality; the triumphant impulse of carnal appetite and the tendency to moralise; the grossness of a mind wholly self-centred, and sudden flashes of almost visionary poetry (*tiny she looked on the grating—that oily, treacly sea*), dishonesty and sincere acceptance of the authority of religion; the whole so organically interwoven and so dominated by the fundamental character of uncompromising pride and tyrannical will. How this will triumphs, how this pride exults at the thought of its last monstrous command! Such may have been the frame of mind of those Saxon warriors and Norsemen, never heard of by this Liverpool parvenu, whose death demanded the slaughter on their tombs of their slaves and horses.

To the coarse and powerful figure of Sir Anthony Gloster may be opposed that of M'Andrew, the first engineer, of whom the old ship-owner said that " he couldn't lie if you paid him, and he'd starve before he stole." He, too, reveals himself to us in a long soliloquy, the finest poem in *The Seven Seas*, and one of Kipling's masterpieces. No character in his tales or novels is the result of a conception more complete or of a creative act more direct and unerring. The poem is only seven pages long, but a living soul appears, and its depths are gradually fathomed. We see more than its present —all the past which has prepared and conditioned that present—those years of bygone life that line a face and mark a character, each trait related to all the others by that organic necessity which the artist perceives in the flashlight of insight. And in like manner everything is of a piece in the poem where this soul expresses itself ; the language, dour and harsh, never coarse ; the style, tense and imperative, never brutal ; the sombre colour, the strong metre of seven feet—a long, tense metre, stretched out, so to speak, by the stress and the movement of the thought. Nor is the impression it conveys that of mass, but of pure, active energy—a difference of the same order as the contrast between the two men. The poet shows but their souls, yet such is his magic that the physical appearance and temperament of each is suggested : the bulk and the thick jowl of the ship-owner, a bovine, sanguine creature (remember he dies of an apoplectic fit), portly as the traditional John Bull ; and in contrast to this, the straight, lean, bony figure, the long, yellow, expressive face, the deep-set eyes of the old Scottish engineer who talks but to himself. Strength of will is the motive power in both, but whereas in the one it is aggressive and almost physical, partaking of brute force, and with the material world as its one object to be subdued and taken possession of, in the other it is secret, inward and spiritual, intent on itself and submitting itself to an ideal. Such a man has not " arrived," has never conquered or mastered any one but himself. His mind is his kingdom, and in his stern soliloquy conscience speaks.

It is night in an engine room, in the depths of his steamer, beating up from the other side of the globe, and coming to the end of her northward voyage. England is nearing, the lights of Ushant flicker out : a dark sky, a quiet sea. The old chief engineer is on watch in the midst of his machinery. No sound but the powerful, regular beat which seems the only thing alive at this time of night, as though there was not a human soul on board. Nothing to be seen but the fixed or rhythmic glitter of metal, the inexorable, gliding return of enormous masses of steel, the accurate and patient concert of a thousand parts, the distributed forces of which gather together in a single thrust the power of seven thousand horses. In the presence of this power, disciplined for service, the Scottish Calvinist, whose soul is all rigorism and certitude, meditates and is moved. What a symbol it all is of the world ordained by the supreme Will for predestined ends, of life regulated by conscience and inflexibly devoted to its prescribed tasks ! The great supple rods rise and return ; the giant cranks, the rocking link-heads repeat their indefatigable round ; the valves quiver, the shaft turns, and the man is set dreaming on this harmony, this persistent labour : " interdependence absolute, foreseen, ordained, decreed, to work, ye'll note, at any tilt an' every rate o' speed."

For to his exacting conscience everything here speaks of duty and effort, everything repeats the lesson he has learnt from his Bible : " Law, Orrder, Duty an' Restraint, Obedience, Discipline "—the rule to which his life has been subdued. And in the long vigil during which he is alone with this bright, active, all-powerful steel he reviews that life and its effort, his sins, the stains of which are black upon his soul, the pride and weakness of his youth, the nights when coming up on deck he would watch the couples lurking between the funnels, his follies in port, his backsliding at Gay

Street in Hong Kong, the voluptuous suggestions of the Tropics under velvet skies and soft, lascivious stars, the voice of the Devil whispering vile things in the perfumed breeze; finally, his fall and long misery until that night in Torres Straits, when as he lay drowsing on the hatch, sick with doubt and fatigue, God spoke to him through the rattle of the anchor chain running out on the coral reef—a voice " clear as our gongs," which he heard thrice repeating : " *Better the sight of eyes that see than wanderin' o' desire.*" It was grace and light upon duty, bright as the carbons in the engine room. " I've lost it since a thousand times, but never past return."

From this moment, order reigns in the man's soul. What has happened is in the nature of that psychological " crystallisation " by which Stendhal explains the birth of love—a crystallisation which at first may sometimes break up, but will always reform again. One must read the poem to the end to see it fixed definitively in all its rigid precision.

The trait is characteristic of these English. Psychologically, they are the very opposite of the shifting, impressionable Russians of Turgenev and Dostoyevsky. All youth is fluid, but an English boy always ends by finding himself and developing a character ; it may be noble or vulgar, simple or complex, but it persists under all influences from without, and through all changes of environment. Between a Sir Anthony Gloster and a M'Andrew there is no kinship, but in both, the power to resist and the unity of the soul are ensured by fixed habits of thought and feeling. The man remains himself, sure of the road he has chosen. This is character and will.

IV.—THE ETHICS OF KIPLING

From this type of soul, common to Kipling's creations, his most individual and self-expressive poetry seems to proceed, and hence its tonic quality. Here a real person is being revealed, an active, durable self traversed by dynamic currents which guide it ever on and are passed on to us. By this feature Kipling, unique in so many respects, is akin to Carlyle, Ruskin, and Tennyson, and if we go further back for his like, Milton, grave, noble, and steadfast, appears, in spite of all differences due to period and culture, as the perfect example of the type.

In such souls the great principle of stability is a conviction born of their own strength, like the deep root grown by a vigorous plant. As with these masters, so with Kipling. His basis is a faith of the same kind as theirs.

We must linger here awhile, for it is the substance of this faith which colours the flower of his poetry. So great an artist was revealed from the outset, he produced such an effect of power as a master of imagery, that at first only his magic was seen ; but under all his fancy and observation a certitude declares itself as fervent as his vision of the universe is intense and true. This energy, alike of conviction and sensation, this attention to spiritual values, together with these powers of vision and imagination, are peculiar to Kipling.

More often than not he expresses himself by images, designed to suggest or awaken a belief. Underlying the obvious meaning of the tale or poem there is another—sometimes, indeed, there are several—more or less interwoven, one of which, however, is essential. He loves to veil his innermost thought thus, and this tendency to symbolism, manifest from the beginning, has increased noticeably in his work. The reason is that his thought has grown deeper, turning gradually from without to within. No doubt such is the general progress of life, the outer world remaining the same about us, but the actual movement of life, the continuous accumulation of memories, adding ever more to our inner world. More and more with this poet, superficially described as a realist, the visible is subordinated to the invisible, sometimes symbolising it, sometimes disappearing altogether. Then, colour and images are suppressed. The idea emerges, stark, direct and compact in its nakedness. There is a flash as of a blade leaping from a scabbard, the rich and vivid chasing of which we had been idly admiring.

This idea, with shades peculiar to a poet born under an alien star, is the old, stern, Puritan, English idea of duty, which inspired so many poets and novelists of the Victorian age, and had already found such strong expression at other periods of English literature. " No nation," says Voltaire, writing about 1750, " has treated of ethics more vigorously and profoundly in poetry than the English." [1] Now that the critical spirit has at last made its way into England, Kipling,

[1] *Siècle de Louis XIV.*, xxxiv.

of all the great living writers of his country, stands alone for the absolute in ethics, with a militant faith. A Wells, a Shaw, a Bennett, a Galsworthy, serve other gods, the gods of reason or of sentiment. Kipling's work appeals to our will, in order to nourish it with the tonic influences we have noted, and also to direct it. For he is not merely the teacher of energy his early works announced ; he is the teacher of *conduct*—a weighty word in English !

Conduct : would he concern himself so much with it, if, with the disciples of Rousseau, he believed that human nature is good, that we have only to trust it, and are excused by our instincts ? The old Christian idea, into which the Reformation had instilled new life, works strongly within him : we must not follow our bent, we must fight against it ; or, as we should say to-day in Bergsonian terms, we must follow the upward movement of life, which strives, against the descending current of things, to concentrate energy in forms ever more complex.

This is the very idea which, more or less clearly defined, inspired the great English moralists of the nineteenth century. Ruskin expresses it clearly, showing duty as a principle making for life, that is to say, for form, that is to say, for beauty, whence the perpetual tendency of his æsthetics towards ethics,— the two points of view being in reality the same. To the author of *The Stones of Venice*, the ethics of a given species is the law demanded by its type, the total of those purifying disciplines which, in the individual, as in society, ensure and increase energy by perfecting the organic form. Thus understood, morality is no mere matter of rules and interdictions. Its idea is not negative ; it is not to be confused with that of a code for the preservation of the established order, with the notion of what is safe and respectable ; one is not tempted to despise it as essentially " middle-class." It is a living, dynamic idea, inspiring enthusiasm ; a vehemence of divine essence and origin, partaking of the driving force of the world ; and just as it possessed the prophets of ancient Israel, it may now pass into the soul of a poet. A religious vehemence, for in Anglo-Saxon countries it is the main element of religion, so much so, that when dogma tends to disappear, it is found all-sufficient in churches which, by their system of collective discipline and practice, seek to maintain the fervour and authority proper to dogma.[1]

Hence the lyrical intensity which often surprises us in the preaching of Carlyle and Ruskin, as in the more ethical poems of Wordsworth and Tennyson—those, in fact, which the English public has always loved. For this public responds to such accents ; more than any other is it sensitive to an order of beauty that appeals only to the soul ; and this we recognise when we reproach our neighbours for looking upon art as a vehicle for moral ideas. More than any other is this public capable of grave enthusiasm for spiritual grandeur, and of this the leaders of the nation are aware ; they know by what bare, stern words, even by what

[1] This is the tendency of the Broad Church party, the Unitarians, and, to-day, even of the Salvation Army. It is very general in America. The Presbyterian Church of Seattle is the most complete example.

silence or injunctions to silence, it may be stirred to
its depths.[1] Is it not a significant fact that in 1897
when Kipling had already published so much that was
moving, nothing of his work had ever thrilled all
England so generally and deeply as those solemn
stanzas of prayer and meditation which he wrote on
the morrow of the Jubilee, under the title of *Recessional*,
a word used in the Anglican service for the subdued
music of the organ when the white-robed clergy and
choristers leave the chancel in slow procession? After
the pomp, the shouting, the blare of trumpets, came
this moving reminder of God and the nothingness of
human dust—*lest we forget! lest we forget!* Five short
stanzas, suggesting a congregation rapt in prayer, and
an effect such as no modern poet had produced upon a
nation. But this was the nation of which Matthew
Arnold was able to say, that its culture proceeds from
the Hebrew mind rather than from Greek thought,
from the Reformation rather than from the Renaissance,
and that it is less concerned with thought and intelligence than with conduct.

Conduct : that is to say, free obedience to a recognised law ; resistance against the world and against
oneself ; perseverance, which is strength—that strength
we have felt in so many of Kipling's creations, expressed
by the rhythm, the style and tone of his poetry. A
virile poetry, the poetry of a soul " four-square to all
the winds that blow," secure in its structure and foundations, proof against the impulse of caprice and all that

---

[1] See Lord Kitchener's proclamations asking for volun-
teers. *Cf.* our earlier book *Britain and the War.*

makes for languor and disintegration. This is true
will power, the basic element in that perfection which
the English have made their ideal, the main object of
education in their public schools, which they express
by one word : *character*.

This perfection is reached when autonomous will
has chosen duty as its goal. To an Englishman of
the fine old type—the regular classic type moulded by
the public schools—whose training was to fit him for
practical life and social service—ideals now no longer
unquestioned—this is the supreme virtue. Intelligence
he is apt to look upon as a whim of nature, a will-of-
the-wisp lighting haphazard on an individual ; a
dangerous light when it shows him his prejudices, and
incites him to discuss those necessary rules of conduct
which have nothing to do with reasoning. But in a
steadfast will, subduing itself to duty, he sees the outcome of ancient culture. Self-knowledge, self-rever-
ence, self-control, these alone raise life to sovereign
power, declared Tennyson, in verses all schoolboys in
his country learn by heart. Of the three words, the
last, *self-control*, is the most English. And the lesson
is almost the same as that suggested to M'Andrew by
the patient, true, well-concerted action of his engines :
" Law, Orrder, Duty an' Restraint, Obedience, Discipline . . ."

What this voluntary submission to strict discipline
should be, the poem which bears as title the little word
If will tell us. It is an exact and rigorous code, in the
simplest language, of the laws a man must obey if he
would be strong against the world and against himself :

RUDYARD KIPLING

If you can keep your head when all about you
Are losing theirs and blaming it on you,
If you can trust yourself when all men doubt you
But make allowance for their doubting, too ;
If you can wait and not be tired of waiting,
Or being lied about don't deal in lies,
Or being hated don't give way to hating
And yet don't look too good, nor talk too wise.

If you can dream—and not make dreams your master ;
If you can think—and not make thoughts your aim ;
If you can meet with Triumph and Disaster
And treat those two impostors just the same ;
If you can bear to hear the truth you've spoken
Twisted by knaves to make a trap for fools,
Or watch the things you gave your life to broken
And stoop and build 'em up with worn-out tools.

If you can make one heap of all your winnings,
And risk it on one turn of pitch and toss,
And lose, and start again at your beginnings,
And never breathe a word about your loss ;
If you can force your nerve and heart and sinew
To serve your turn long after they have gone,
And so hold on when there is nothing in you
Except the will which says to you : " Hold on ! "

If you can talk with crowds and keep your virtue,
Or walk with Kings—nor lose the common touch,
If neither foes nor loving friends can hurt you,
If all men count with you, but none too much ;
If you can fill the unforgiving minute
With sixty seconds' worth of distance run,
Yours is the Earth and everything that's in it
And—which is more—you'll be a Man, my son.[1]

[1] *If,* at the end of *Brother Square-Toes,* in *Rewards and Fairies.*

Such perfection is indeed rare—an ideal towards which one may strive without ever reaching it. But it is precisely this, the tendency or direction, which interests us here, for it shows one of the two great cultural ideas that have prevailed in England—individualism. The effort must bear first upon ourselves. To govern and direct oneself, to be a man, a man self-governing and responsible for his acts, the " captain of his soul," is the first commandment of School and Church, still more emphatically expressed by the official liturgy in the exhortation to the Sovereign at the Coronation : " Be strong and play the man." Of course, the maxim taken in its deeper sense is of religious Protestant origin. It implies the autonomy of individual conscience, which no rite, no intermediary, can relieve of the burden of sin, but only the steadfast, effectual pursuit of self-reformation and discipline. Let each be on his guard against intrusions from without, for nothing can absolve a man from the task of self-guidance. Thus the Puritan rule threw man back upon himself by isolating him before God, and the political idea of self-government was reinforced by a religious idea. Such was the moral principle of that individualism, once supposed to be the whole of the English character, though, as a fact, it is but its foundation.

For self-command is not all. What should the soul obey ? How is this strong man, described as " lord of himself," and, so, of all things, to apply his strength ? We shall better understand the English poet's creed if we illustrate it by a contrast, and recall other ideals expressed in other literatures by masters whose influence has endured for generations. It was this contrast which astonished Taine when, in the 'sixties, he compared Tennyson and Alfred de Musset, and the modern English poets and novelists in general with their French contemporaries, even with those whose genius he had most loved and praised. These, from Chateaubriand down to Baudelaire, were also for the most part individualists, but with a difference. With them the *ego* kept itself strong only for its own sake. It was itself it worshipped when they professed scorn of rules and conventions, and these they could magnificently cast to the winds in their imaginary world. Their heroes either fled from society or undertook to conquer it. They soared above and beyond all laws. When to a Julian Sorel the idea of *duty* presented itself, it was in an inverted form.[1] True, the effect of such teaching on morals is not necessarily all that might be supposed. Nevertheless, in the ordinary course of life, when no public danger suddenly draws men together, it tends to divest the idea of duty of its social character and confine it to one's own self. In some instances (Goethe is a magnificent example) duty will mean the projection upon one's mind of an image of the universe ever richer and truer ; in many others it will be to project upon others an image, ever more brilliant and seductive, of oneself. According to the formulas of the age, the first seek to " develop " themselves,

[1] See Stendhal's *Le Rouge et le Noir*, Vol. I., pp. 51, 54, 77, 85, concerning the seduction of Madame de Rénal considered as a " duty," a " painful " and " heroic " duty.

the second to " arrive." But for all alike the motive power is an imperious, absorbing discipline, demanding renunciation, self-control, continuous and methodical effort, and thus presenting itself all the more evidently as duty.

Very different is the idea of which Kipling is the apostle. To a certain extent it is derived from the Puritan tradition—from remembrance of the Ten Commandments ; hence, at times, its solemn and imperative accent. But it springs, above all, from that social instinct which in Anglo-Saxon countries has dedicated so much effort, so many lives and fortunes, to the future of the hive and of the race. For the Englishman, who calls himself an individualist, is nevertheless a creature of the hive, essentially a political animal. This antinomy is not rare in life ; it is to be found, in varying proportions of its two terms, in men of all nations. Perhaps the social, or, maybe, the merely gregarious element now tends to predominate in each soul, as a result of the new civilisation, which accelerates and multiplies the currents of ideas and feelings—but this does not mean that the old imperatives necessary to collective life have strengthened their hold upon the individual, for there are other influences at work in these days to diminish their prestige.

Yet they are still very strong in England, manifesting themselves in traits which foreigners have always been quick to notice ; as, for instance, in the old habit of association for ends demanded by what our neighbours call public spirit. For such is the essentially practical form of the social instinct in the English ; they draw

together, not so much to share in the animation of a
concourse of men, as to co-operate in a work they have
conceived or made their own.   In activities of this kind,
two principles apparently antagonistic are reconciled.
The enterprise is born of an individual movement of
mind or conscience ; but it aims at some benefit for
the group, and to promote this, men combine their
efforts.   To the English this is the social act proper,
for which the school seeks to prepare the young by its
games and rules.   And because the social instinct is
so strong in Kipling he insists on the discipline of self-
sacrifice and submission which makes it possible.

Note also that his mind is one of those which look at
things from the point of view of organisation, seeing in
a living whole the sum of life rather than the elements,
and in a community the secular collective being rather
than the short-lived individual.   Here again he reminds
us of Carlyle and Ruskin, those teachers of a political
philosophy known in England as Social Toryism.
And, indeed, if the word *Socialism* had its literal sense,
meaning a doctrine which really places the State above
the man, or a certain category of men, it might be
applied to minds of this cast.   But they are Tories ;
their movement is opposed to the so-called democratic
idea, an outcome of the Liberal idea, which tends to
release the individual from the ancient sanctions and
prejudices invented in the course of ages by the life
instinct of the group: " I am an *illiberal*," said Ruskin.

For in their eyes the principle of society is not the
right of the individual, but his duty.   Man was made
for the community, they think, not the community for

man, and the elementary act by which it is constituted and maintained takes place, not when he asserts his right, but when he devotes himself to his duty. My right is what is due to me ; if I claim it, I place myself apart. This is a centripetal idea, anarchic in its essence ; it tends to dissociate. My duty is what I owe to others ; when I give myself to it, I give myself to them, I adhere, I collaborate. This is a centrifugal idea, of the synthetic and organic order ; it constructs and combines. Is it not a significant fact that since Rousseau, who boasted that he obeyed only his heart and never his duty, Romantics and Democrats have joined forces to proclaim—the first in the name of feeling and passion, the second in the name of reason—the right of nature and of the individual as against the traditional prohibitions and conventions of society ?

Romanticism has always existed in England, but the anti-social principle latent in it, so swiftly manifested in the lives and works of Shelley and Byron, was soon eliminated. Reaction against the French Revolution, the accession to power of an industrial *bourgeoisie* brought up in the Puritan tradition, the Evangelical revival, the moral influence of Queen Victoria, and, above all, the strong English sense of the conditions of social health were so many hindrances to its development, whereas on the Continent Byron's influence went on spreading and deepening.

The same for democracy. Our neighbours have always had something of it since the eighteenth century —and indeed the struggle for rights and liberties became a ruling principle in the life of the English at

a very early date. But at the historical moment which
decided the modern trend of the English mind,·the
individual was mainly concerned with liberty to obey
his own conscience, with his right to do those things
which he ought to do, and to leave undone those things
which he ought not to do—in other words, the right of
duty conceived as such ; by which I mean as an act
self-imposed, not enforced from without, as formerly in
Germany by the State. This was the idea prevalent in
England, a heritage of her Puritan past, when she
began her democratic evolution. So general and so
imperative is it, that when the English follow their
egotistical tendency, which is strong, they have first
to persuade themselves that they are obeying their
conscience—one has always to reckon with the recru-
descence of this simple and powerful illusion. Hence the
old accusation of hypocrisy which nations more tolerant
of human frailty (our neighbours say, more cynical)
have so often brought against England—an indirect
testimony to the prestige still attached in that country
to the idea of moral obligation. I do not maintain
that the efficacy of this idea will always endure, and
that it will indefinitely survive dogmas which are its
support and substance. But as long as it does persist,
what a principle of *self-government* it is, what a correc-
tive for a political system, the evident danger of which
is the organised reign of individual appetites !

But English democracy is a strange thing. However
" advanced " it may be, however deeply stirred in its
masses by new ideas, it remains imbued with religious,
and indeed, pietistic, thought and sentiment—while on

the other hand, by a paradox which a keen native observer pronounced incomprehensible to a foreigner, elements of aristocratic origin are recognisable in its habits and ideals. " A democracy of aristocrats," says Kipling, confirming this view. And the same lack of logic is apparent in the Constitution. For if the government of the people by the people has always had its champions on the other side of the Channel, universal suffrage is an institution of yesterday, and England has still her House of Lords Spiritual and Temporal, her law of primogeniture, and her wealthy Established Church dating from the Middle Ages—its head a King whose moral authority has something sacred to which the presence of the golden mace in Parliament testifies. Broadly speaking, Great Britain began her revolution barely ten years ago. One had to wait for the critical movement started by the Boer War to see great writers enter upon campaigns comparable—however different the time, the scene and methods—to those initiated in France by Hugo in *Les Misérables*, Michelet in *Le Peuple*, and George Sand in *Indiana*.

In the midst of these new manifestations Kipling's work appears as the last great outcrop of the underlying granite, the profound moral basis of England.

* * *

Never, perhaps, did the thought he in his turn transmits present itself in a form so English. It is so concrete, so spontaneous, so young with the eternal youth of instinct, so responsive to the fervid sense of social and national life that inspired it. Indeed, the word *duty* is too abstract to render its leading idea. For this word

RUDYARD KIPLING

—the *Leitmotiv* of English poetry and the English novel
in the nineteenth century—the author of *The Five
Nations* substitutes the simpler and more social term
service, evoking the familiar notion of each man's
work and the daily task he performs in common with
others.

This is one of his recurrent themes, attesting that
worship of practical values shared by Englishmen of
so many different types and periods : by a Bacon as by
an Addison and a Defoe, by a Sydney Smith and a
Macaulay as by a Carlyle and a Ruskin. There are
winged spirits—the dreamer, the thinker, the genius—
who soar to the empyrean. They see what we cannot
see, but they dwell apart. Not among these does our
poet seek his kin. And here he reveals the warm
humanity of a mind we might have supposed to be
purely aristocratic and stoical. Those he loves, those
he claims as his brethren, are the men who toil together
with other men, the " Sons of Martha," as distinguished
from the " Sons of Mary "—all those obscure millions
whose daily labour strengthens and augments the
achievement of our race, lifting the deadweight of
things, and fighting the forces of decay.

It is their care in all the ages to take the buffet and
    cushion the shock.
It is their care that the gear engages ; it is their care
    that the switches lock.
It is their care that the wheels run truly ; it is their
    care to embark and entrain,
Tally, transport and deliver duly the Sons of Mary by
    land and main.

They say to mountains, " Be ye removed." They say
    to the lesser floods, " Be dry."
Under their rods are the rocks reproved—they are not
    afraid of that which is high.
Then do the hill-tops shake to the summit—then is the
    bed of the deep laid bare
That the Sons of Mary may overcome it, pleasantly
    sleeping and unaware.

They finger Death at their gloves' end where they piece
    and repiece the living wires.
IIe rears against the gates they tend ; they feed him
    hungry behind their fires.
Early at dawn, ere men see clear, they stumble into his
    terrible stall,
And hale him forth like a haltered steer, and goad and
    turn him till evenfall.

They do not preach that their God will rouse them a
    little before the nuts work loose.
They do not teach that His Pity allows them to leave
    their work when they damn well choose.
As in the thronged and lighted ways, so in the dark and
    the desert they stand
Wary and watchful all their days that their brethren's
    days may be long in the land.

And all these, rich or poor, are the men who do the
work for which they draw the wage, men of the forge,
the mine, the bench, the deck, the mill, the school, the
battalion, the counter, the trench, the rail, the sheepfold, the Senate, ay, and the throne (*save he serve no
man may rule*—), all the good workers who pay the
daily debt by their high courage, who untiringly begin,
continue and finish the task for which they draw the
wage.

RUDYARD KIPLING

In such men the creator of Mulvaney and M'Andrew sees a beauty born of the work which has gradually shaped and directed their whole being. He sees them marked with that strong professional stamp which he himself has shown us in the sharp modelling of the many soldiers, officers, engineers, officials, journalists, artisans, sailors, business men who people his tales. And he sees in them not only beauty but joy—the organic joy born of assured poise and complete adjustment—each man loving his task, whose rhythms have become part of his life, needing it as he needs his daily bread or his pay ; thinking more of it than of his wage, and deriving from it more than from his wage, his sense of his mission and his dignity.[1] In our modern world there are, of course, tasks in which a man can find no such satisfactions, and in the humiliation born of these, as Ruskin tells us, the hatred and revolt of slaves are bred. But in the camps of India, on the sea, in the farms of Canada and the Cape, as in the Sussex weald, Kipling had seen more especially those old unchanging callings to which the soul brings its share of pride, faithfulness and courage, and in the exercise of which the humblest—peasant, artisan or soldier—is conscious of skill and value—callings in which the disciplined body attains that dignity we admire in the strong arm of the blacksmith shaping the iron, and the straining muscles of the sailor hauling with his mates. A seaman at his post in the crew of a fishing smack, with the fierce, restless, infinite powers round him, would be to this poet an apt symbol of man in society, and of society

[1] *Cf.* Ruskin, *Unto this Last*, I.

81

in Nature. On such a vessel there is none, from cabin
boy to captain, who has not learnt to serve in the
pitiless school of the sea ; none who does not owe to
others his just, exact and daily meed of service.

In all ranks of society these are the men he admires
and respects. These, too, Carlyle reverenced ; the men
who *can*, as the sage of Chelsea said in mystic accents,
those whose labour breaks through the blind concatena-
tion of necessities, to modify, or rather to create the
real—the creators of facts—true men. And even less
free than the rest, those whose task is leadership, who
" launch the van straight at the grinning teeth of
things," and daily lift " their souls, their cause, their
clan a little from the ruck of things "—a Rhodes, a
Milner, a Chamberlain, a Roberts, an Edward VII.
But in the lower spheres, as in the higher, there is no
true service that does not demand the gift of oneself,
sacrifice to the point of exhaustion, and even of death.
No physical beauty of joyous adaptation then, but
supreme spiritual beauty and contentment of the man
who does not yield, because he has taken his stand in
the citadel of his soul. He has returned to that secret
individualism, the root of which is the deep-seated and
jealous idea of a self-governing and responsible conscience.[1]

Thus understood, service is the vital principle of a
society, and the spontaneous imperative by which the

[1] These ideas are further developed in *Things and the
Man*, and *The Pro-Consuls* in *The Years Between*. See also
The Reformers and *Bridge-Guard* in *The Five Nations*, and
The Ship that found herself in *Traffics and Discoveries*.

individual imposes it upon himself is the law of general life speaking in him. Such a law, Kipling would say, if he used Spencerian terms, expresses a tendency similar to that of healthy cells to function in a given organism. When this tendency decreases, we say that the tissues are growing old or degenerating. It is the same with a people in whom the will to serve is weakening. Here the poet's idea is akin to Burke's view of society as seen by the lurid light of the French Revolution, an idea Joseph de Maistre revived when he showed the social body as a mystic whole, the resistance and cohesion of which are assured, through the millions of deaths and births, by a principle not of the rational order. Only for Kipling the virtue which brings about this miracle is not the obscure prestige of ancient institutions, but the elementary act which may be called the reflex of duty.

This virtue it has become more and more his mission to defend and quicken in the English community. If it still works so strongly in him, if he remains impervious to influences which now lead so many writers in his country to declare for the individual as against collective discipline, this is due not only to a natural disposition, but also to the unforgettable lesson he has learned in British India. In the torrid country where he began to be a man there is not an Englishman, he tells us, who lives but for himself. In many famous stories he has shown us how strong is the idea of professional duty here, how true the loyalty of the man to his task and his team, how steadfast the sentiment that devotes an administrator to his struggle against famine, a

83

doctor to his struggle against disease, a journalist to his newspaper, an officer to his regiment, a sailor to his ship. He has shown us effort maintained to exhaustion, to the breaking point, and sacrifice culminating in death, the threat of which is never far distant in times of cholera, or in summer, when " the well is dry beneath the village tree, the river but a belt of blinding sand, the earth is iron, and the skies are brass."

And the significant trait in these stories is that this faithfulness to one's task is taken for granted; no extraordinary events occur in which the idea of duty is heightened. Simply the man must do what he must do; everything incites, compels him to the required action—his instincts, his surroundings, the customs and opinions which life and education have made his—himself, in short, his nature reinforced by his whole culture. He cannot help himself : when the idea of duty has been grasped, all the rest follows as inevitably as the march of fate. Duty here appears as the English form of fatality.

That fate the poet himself obeyed. It is no mere invention of the intellect which finds expression in so many poems, scenes, images and pictures of lively, active figures. A religion is at work, an atavic habit of the soul, an inevitable and irreducible manner of feeling and willing which his aim is not so much to define as to communicate. Men should live, and induce others to live according to the Law, as in the symbolic Jungle, where Law reigns, and not, as some have said, Force. Of all the inhabitants of the Jungle, the strongest, the insolent Shere Khan, is a brigand, outlawed because he set himself above all laws. He will be vanquished by the alliance of all, as will also happen to a certain nation that has become too strong in the human Jungle. This poet has presentiments of this kind.

In short, if Kipling were to formulate his refusal to philosophise in philosophic terms, he would say something like this :

In the English hive a system of rules and ideas prevails. This, for an Englishman, is the basis of all things. No doubt one could imagine another of a scientific, abstract sort, founded upon some universal theorem. The English care little for these things, they do not dwell in the lonely world of pure thought. Let the Celts (there are some in Britain) or the Slavs follow an idea until it takes them out of their group and they see it from outside. Let them destroy their world that they may build on absolute truth. The Englishman is part of the system that has made him what he is ; he cannot dissociate himself from it. He does not question it ; he lives it.

And because he lives it, his art and his poetry inevitably express it.

* * *

We can see now the unity of Kipling's thought and recognise its organic and, therefore, necessary sequence. His sense of the bond that links him to the community governs everything—the consecration of his powers as an artist to truths he considered vital, his untiring attention to his country's peril, his social conception, his political leanings, his ethics—his very religion.

And we can also better understand the origin and meaning of his Imperialism. Because he is so keenly alive to the order and harmony in the mutual relations of a living whole, because the sense of obligation is so strong in him, he assigns to the English nations in the Empire, and to the Empire in mankind that function of service which he deems the *raison d'être* of the individual in the nation. Just as Englishmen had founded their community on the rights of individuals, so they founded the Empire on the rights of the English peoples—and such were these rights that politically there was no Empire. Of these rights, the first for each of these peoples was to govern itself, for itself alone, with a view to its own personal success ; each remaining absolutely independent of the other. And as Kipling, on the other hand, conceived of society as founded on duty, on duty he wished to base the Empire. Duty here is what the poet would call, in simple English fashion, playing for the team. For, broadly speaking, this is an extension to nations of the team idea, or, to borrow a comparison of which Kipling has made a fine tale, the hive idea. There is a British Empire : let each British nation become conscious of the fact and of her debt to this greater community. In Imperialism of this kind, the main idea is not that of *imperium*, but that of an imperative—of duty as between the clans.

Or even, to go to the root of the matter, of duty pure and simple, for beyond the ethics peculiar to the hive, there is another moral code, more general and universal, religious in its origin, on which every English conscience is nourished. It forms part of the system and its laws take precedence of all others. Here we have the essential difference between the English and the German hive. To the German, the State is absolute—in all matters that affect its interests it can change the definition of right and wrong; when the State commands, the human being is but its creature. To the English one thing alone is absolute—the distinction between right and wrong, a fixed principle in the law of his hive, and binding on all mankind. To use another familiar English phrase, we may say that if one of their watchwords is " play for the team," there is another of even greater import—" play the game "; play it, that is to say, according to the rules recognised by all teams—positive rules, which do not merely forbid, but prescribe. Beyond what Englishmen and the British peoples owe to the Empire, these rules set forth what the Empire owes to the subject races and to mankind :

> Keep ye the Law—be swift in all obedience—
> Clear the land of evil, drive the road and bridge the ford.
> Make ye sure to each his own
> That he reap where he hath sown ;
> By the peace among our peoples let men know we serve
>   the Lord.[1]

To serve God, in the language of the Anglo-Saxons, both in America and in England, where religion inclines more and more to pragmatism, means to serve man, to quicken the movement of life against the passiveness of things, to construct, to organise, to battle against poverty, suffering, ignorance, sloth, injustice—all that makes for suffering and degeneracy.

[1] *Song of the English* in *The Seven Seas.*

ENGLISH LITERATURE

To the Englishman in India, as to the American in the Philippines, it means to " take up the white man's burden," to be patient and self-forgetful, to accept the part of " serf and sweeper, to seek another's profit, to fill the mouth of Famine and bid the sickness cease." It means to hand on to the native the knowledge and power of the European until he himself can make his own law and obey it.[1]

Such is the task of England in that India where under the British Raj justice weighs the rights of great and small in the same scales, where Mussulman and Hindu no longer massacre each other periodically, where the famines which used to destroy millions have become rare and manageable. In one of his tales, Kipling has told us what devotion may be brought to the campaign against this scourge by British civil servants—by English women, who belong to no service but who are moved by the spirits of a Florence Nightingale and an Edith Cavell.[2] This devotion does not spring from the English instinct of the hive, but from a higher authority—that conscience the poet addressed in the Prelude to his war poems, when he shows us the Tempter offering Man Glory and Power, and bidding him shape the Kingdom to his mind, for his will can give him all things. " ' But the Kingdom—the Kingdom is within you,' said the Man's own Mind to the Man."[3]

Here we come to religion. Its tones are constantly

[1] *The White Man's Burden* in *The Five Nations.*
[2] *William the Conqueror* in *The Day's Work.*
[3] *Dedication* in *The Years Between.*

88

recurring in Kipling's poetry, and not only its tones, but its very language, the solemn language of the Liturgy. We have already met it. The foreigner who has not been brought up from childhood on the Scriptures in the old English fashion cannot feel its full power. It is like some fundamental strain in a symphony, graver and more moving than all the rest, which his ear misses. Not only does he lack a knowledge of the particular verse quoted or alluded to by the poet, but since the archaic diction that gives this language its peculiar character disappears in a translation the solemnity of the English text is lost to him. All that reaches him is the idea, stripped of its religious halo, those purple gleams with which style, phraseology and rhythms invest it for the English reader.

But there must be no mistake as to the significance of such language in this poetry and in English poetry generally. It is heard whenever the moral idea attains a certain height, and conscience is sufficiently moved. For to an Englishman the sense of the Law, of the things he should do and the things he should not do is associated with the accents of the Bible, and the stern, bare vehemence of the Commandments. The lyrical quality latent in the English idea of duty is to be explained by the profound influence of the Book in which the Law is the main principle of religion, and speaks in such solemn language.

In what may be called Anglo-Saxon Christianity, the Law is also the essential principle, and if we except the Ritualistic movement in the High Church, it tends to become all-important. In the religion implied in

Kipling's poetry, as in that which Carlyle formerly translated in terms of philosophy, this end seems to have been achieved. Duty here appears as the ultimate, immovable reality beyond the flux of things and beings. Here we have the dogmatic, substantial, European element of his thought.

And yet he has lived too long in India not to see thickening around him the bewildering fumes in which the matter of the world dissolves. His Kim, into whom he has projected something of his own childhood, and whose soul is dual, at once Eastern and Western, experiences strange moments in which his substance, his very self, seems to leave him, to melt into space and appear as a dream. Some of the first tales had given us to an almost intolerable degree the feeling of annihilation, of the nothingness into which vanishes all that was beauty, youth, passion, exultation in life—that life which cannot really conceive that it may cease to be. It might have been supposed that under a mask of impassibility this triumphant young man was taking a savage delight in trampling and levelling the ground where Death had destroyed the house of Love. People talked of his Nihilism ; and no doubt at this period of his life in India, where the human form dissolving on the burning *ghât* is a daily sight, he may have pondered on the idea of the final *Nada*, the void in which the universal illusion hovers. Some echo of this idea haunted him from the first. Later on, calling up the ages of the past, civilisations and kingdoms that have blossomed and vanished, he reminded us how

RUDYARD KIPLING

> Cities and Thrones and Powers
> Stand in Time's eye
> Almost as long as flowers
> Which daily die.
> But as new buds put forth
> To glad new men,
> Out of the spent and unconsidered earth
> The cities rise again.[1]

The daffodil of to-day knows nothing of the daffodils
before it, and thinks it will live for ever. Just as it is
fading into death,

> Shadow to shadow well persuaded saith :
> See how our works endure !

But though the daffodil fade, at least, while it lasts
it obeys, each one of its million cells obeys, the law
which neither flower nor cell ever invented, chose, or
questioned, and yet must follow, simply because it is
the law, the only reality they know—and because they
follow it, their life and form find a place in the general
order. Thus, accepting Kipling's image, we may
conceive the harmony of the two ideas : that which
denies and that which affirms. The dominant English
idea, that which asserts a law, and which he has
repeated in so many forms, shows itself from the
beginning ; we see it active and embodied in the English
characters of the early tales. It finds complete expression in the poems of *The Seven Seas*, in which the theme
of duty recurs so insistently. The *Recessional* presents
it with its antithesis ; contrasting the immutability of
the law and the evanescence of our world, but under
the Hebraic form—God the Judge appearing behind the

---

[1] *Songs from Books : Dedication.*

law which emanates from Him. All the pomp of the Empire is " one with Nineveh and Tyre," the work of " valiant dust that builds on dust." One thing alone avails—the ancient sacrifice, the submission of the heart to the Law ordained by the Lord.

Such expressions occur fairly often in the poet's work. How far, it may be asked, are they symbolical, how far do they simply repeat forms of speech current in England, especially in those Victorian days when belief in the letter of the Bible was more general than now ? It is not easy to say. An Englishman's religion is often wrapt in a haze of pious sentiment which veils its precise contours, and he himself would be puzzled to define it exactly. It happens sometimes that the kernel is insensibly merged into the chiaroscuro that envelops it. But in most cases the man remains religious. The dogmatic outline of his faith may dissolve more or less, but the substance endures. What he feels, or rather what he perceives with confident emotion is, beyond the dream of life, a mysterious world to which we must look for the reason of duty. With this indefinable, yet certain reality, he communicates by his intimate sense of the Law. Of all he can know, this Law alone partakes of that Absolute, all the forms of which imagined by man are fleeting. Perhaps nothing else is absolute, and this would seem to be the central thought of the poet :

What boots it on the gods to call ?
Since, answered or unheard,
We perish with the gods and all
Things made—except the Word.[1]

[1] *A Recantation* in *The Years Between.*

92

True, the poem in which he speaks thus is overcast by a personal sorrow, one of those griefs with which the war has filled the hearts of so many fathers. But, on the first day of the war, Rudyard Kipling, speaking to the English, and giving utterance to the same thought, used a simpler and more solemn expression—" the Commandments." [1]

V.—THE SONGS: THE LAND AND HER DEAD.

OVER-INSISTENCE on the practical and religious beliefs underlying Kipling's poetry would give a misleading idea of it. Of course they nourish it, and it is essential to know them, for they are the common ground of all English culture. But a ground is a colourless thing, and Kipling's poetry is as diverse and vivid as the blossoms springing from the clay in the course of the seasons.

How are we to suggest this variety, in which we find now the splendour of the East, now the tender and delicate shades of our northern world? The reader will form an idea of it if he glances at the *Songs from Books*. Here we are not looking at flower-beds in which the successive dreams and moods of a poet are arranged according to species and colours, but at the wayward growths that spring up luxuriantly from the April to the September of a life.

These songs are peculiar in their kind. All readers of Kipling know that it has long been his custom to write as a prelude to his stories a few verses that give

[1] *For all we have and are, ibid.*

the tone, and to close them with stanzas, in which the underlying idea is set forth, stripped of the outline, even of the matter proper to the narrative—transmuted into music full of a new magic, and as it were spiritualised. In this collection, the echoes of all the tales he has given to the world for the last twenty years seem to reverberate. A crowd of spirits reappear and press together. And here and there familiar voices call to us, those of Kim, Mowgli, Puck and others, rising above the whispers of the land—of the ancient Indian, and the no less ancient English land : light, infinite sonorities alive with the intermingled waves of music and poetry, with rhythms of lullabies and nursery songs, charms and incantations, Oriental chants and English ballads, hymns and the solemn prayers of the Liturgy—alive with movements of joy, humour, and youthful fancy (childhood itself flits by, full of wonder, delighting in familiar or fabulous beasts, mimicking their ways and language)—with religious impulses, flights of metaphysical imagination, moods of slow and solemn musing ; for in these Englishmen deep earnestness does not preclude unquenchable boyish freshness and vitality.

Most of these poems belong to what may be called Kipling's second period, both art and inspiration being very different from those of *The Seven Seas* or *The Five Nations*. Here we are less conscious of personal energy. Nothing imperious and nothing imperial. The tense, sudden effect, which to some seemed even brutal, has disappeared, together with the strong staccato beat of the metre. Such art no longer startles ;

it penetrates and charms us. So true it is that the genius of a great artist, who is sensitive to all the aspects of life, and has passed through all the changes of life, will not be bound for ever to any formula.

And again, everything here is less direct, for now the poet tries to *suggest* rather than to describe (hence the frequent use of the parenthesis). Memories, forebodings, yearnings are awakened ; they seem to float like echoes left in the soul by the drama the poet has evoked ; or rather, they are felt like emotion in a dream—a dream in which the events of day-time are transfigured and appear in new images of deeper and more solemn meaning. In short, the novelist having treated his theme passes it on to the poet, who does not simply transpose it into verse, but creates anew from it. I know nothing like this in literature.

Of course, to get the full effect, we must begin by reading the narrative—that, for instance, which is called *A Deal in Cotton*. It is the story of a very young colonial official, the head of a lonely outpost in Equatorial Africa, who undertakes to introduce the cotton plant into his district. He is the only white man, with an Indian servant and a little band of negroes under him—so lonely that it has become a habit with him to recite verses aloud to the trees. Round him are cannibals and slave-hunters ; he has to fight and negotiate unceasingly. Meanwhile, his mind is full of his cotton scheme, impossible for lack of money and labour, a scheme which, when fever lays hold of him, becomes an obsession. By a strange chance he has saved an Arab, a wounded slave-trader, with a price

upon his head, whom he did not recognise ; he has
nursed him in his own quarters, and won his heart.
While the young man lies delirious, the slaver makes
use of his prestige with a tribe of cannibals and gets
from them men and money to start the enterprise.
The first part of the story is told by the hero himself,
on sick leave in England. He is twenty ; he is the son
of the Strickland of the Tales ; he speaks before his
parents and some friends, one of whom was " the
Infant " in the *Conference of the Three Powers*. He
speaks exactly as did the young men of that conference
twenty-five years before, elliptically, in humorous
slangy jargon, and only in answer to the friends who
assail him with questions, for, from one generation to
the next, the same spirit has passed. When he has
finished, his mother, who has been listening with
shining eyes, takes him away to bed and quinine. The
reader, carried away by the story, needs all his attention
to perceive the little touches by which the writer has
suggested what is to him the essential theme, the man's
secret and enthusiastic devotion to his task. The poet
now returns to the idea, combining it with new matter
more diffuse and general, and thus transmuted, it
unveils itself under the title : *The New Knighthood.*

> Who gives him the Bath ?
> " I," said the wet
> Rank jungle-sweat,
> " I'll give him the Bath."
> Who'll sing the Psalms ?
> " We," said the Palms,
> " Ere the hot wind becalms,
> We'll sing the Psalms."

Who lays on the sword ?
" I," said the Sun,
" Before he has done
I'll lay on the sword."

Who fastens his belt ?
" I," said Short Rations,
" I know all the fashions
Of tightening a belt."

Who gives him his spur ?
" I," said his Chief,
Exacting and brief,
" I'll give him the spur."

Who'll shake his hand ?
" I," said the Fever,
" And I'm no deceiver,
I'll shake his hand."

Who brings him the Wine ?
" I," said Quinine,
" It's a habit of mine,
I'll come with his wine."

Who'll put him to proof ?
" I," said All Earth,
" Whatever he's worth
I'll put to the proof."

Who'll choose him for Knight ?
" I," said his Mother,
" Before any other,
My very own Knight."

And after this fashion adventure to seek
Was Sir Galahad made—as it might be last week.

*

*   *

Among these songs some seem of peculiar bearing

on the poet's own history. They are the simplest, the
least vivid perhaps, but how instinct with feeling !
The subject is merely the ancient, changeless English
land, and they seem to soar, gray and tremulous as
larks, from the heather and the pale downs of Sussex.

The South African war was over, and Kipling had
just published *The Five Nations* when he was captured
by the secret magic of this countryside, by the spell of
peace it whispers, and all of the ancient ancestral world
that lingers in it for an Englishman. It gave this
great patriot a new vision of his country, a deeper sense
of the tie that binds him to it. Unlike the Englishman
of the island, who belongs at first to his parish, and
whose horizon rarely embraces the whole national
domain, he had begun by knowing the Empire. Roving
the seas, he had found it in all parts of the world. He
had seen but the present of his country, and he had
seen it expanded over the globe. Now that he had
returned to the land of his fathers, and settled, far from
the great highways, in one of those quiet southern
counties where the legends and traditions of old
England have survived, he learned to look at it in the
perspective of the past, and to commune silently with
its deep, abiding soul.

This county of Sussex by the sea is a land of memories. A spell as of the Sleeping Beauty lingers there,
and time seems to have stood still. Nothing happens ;
the country folk, slow, heavy and silent—shepherds,
labourers, millers, charcoal-burners—lead the same
rustic, Christian life as their forbears, to the rhythm of
recurrent works and days. The old men have a wisdom

not to be learnt at school, that comes from the long years of a life given to the things of woods and fields, and beyond that, from the experience of past generations. They never cease working ; they are never ill ; they die suddenly, like a branch that withers and drops one day from the tree. A two hours' journey from London brings one out of the modern world into a region untouched, it would seem, by the eighteenth century, for here we do not find those great domains, which are the distinctive mark left by this period on the English country. The land is much divided : the property of peasants, yeomen, of ancient and simple gentry, people who go a-foot by hidden paths, the intricate network of which reaches everywhere. Small estates that figured in the Conqueror's Domesday Book are still to be found there. The poet's home is grave and simple, built in the time of James I. by an ironmaster, who, if he could revisit it, wearing the ruff of the period, would find there the heavy furniture of polished oak familiar to him, and would not perceive that centuries have slipped by. The house is surrounded by the same terraces, the same pleasaunce, the same fields ; beyond, one sees the dim purple or brown of the thickets which provided the charcoal, the only fuel of the old forges. These have long been extinguished. Nowadays the landscape is more silent than ever, and everything blends into harmony under the patient finger of Time. One feels that human beings and things have endured together in unhasting, monotonous life. There is the same ancient marriage of a certain race and a certain soil as in our Brittany. The magic of this soil, the gentle, irresistible power by which it takes silent possession of men of the race, the memories and secrets it whispers, Kipling, fresh from new worlds and all the lands of the Empire, learned by experience and recorded in one of his tales. We remember that pair of nervous, restless Americans, who, returning by chance to the home of their fathers, are gradually invaded by its strange charm, and are finally held there as by a spell, throwing out, so to speak, invisible roots, whence they draw daily the soothing and mysterious influences of the earth. But in the tale we hear only of the humans who, passing by, are caught unawares by this witchery. In the chant at the end— a poem too slow and meditative to be called a song— the eternal soul of the land itself speaks :

> I am the land of their fathers,
> In me the virtue stays,
> I will bring back my children
> After certain days.
>
> Under their feet in the grasses
> My clinging magic runs.
> They shall return as strangers,
> They shall remain as sons.
>
> Over their heads in the branches
> Of their new-bought ancient trees,
> I weave an incantation
> And draw them to my knees.
>
> Scent of smoke in the evening,
> Smell of rain in the night
> The hours, the days, and the seasons
> Order their soul aright.

RUDYARD KIPLING

Till I make plain the meaning
Of all my thousand years,
Till I fill their hearts with knowledge
While I fill their eyes with tears.[1]

Tears : how new this is to us in Kipling's masculine
poetry ! We have travelled far indeed from the
imperial trumpet-blasts and the organ notes of the
early verse. The music of Empire was attuned to a
will directed towards the future. This is but the
voice of the homeland, a small voice rising from the
depths of the soil and from an immemorial past.
Surely he who is listening to it here with such loving
attention has known the weariness of strange lands,
where day breaks with dazzling swiftness, where
Nature is too sudden and violent and nothing responds
to our deeper inherited yearnings. He seems to have
known the homesickness of which he tells in his Anglo-
Indian stories—

" O the *Heimweh*, ceaseless, aching,
O the black dividing sea and alien plain ! " [2]—

the longing for England and the north, where hours
and seasons change slowly, where, under a gray sky
in the pale endless twilight, a little spire with tinkling
bell, low cottages bowered in honeysuckle harmonise
with drowsy fields—*Scent of smoke in the evening, smell
of rain in the night.* It is as if life, which lays its hand
upon us all, had left its trace upon him who seemed to
us the embodiment of strength, as if he had been

[1] *The Recall* in *An Habitation Enforced.*
[2] *Christmas in India* in *Departmental Ditties.*

softened by a share in common suffering. And how much nearer to us this brings him, how much more deeply he touches our hearts! It seems as if, in this enfolding English scenery, the memory and the need of which had secretly endured in him, he had found at last peace and order. Speaking of the influence of this country just now, I used the word "charm," and this is the very title of the poem that describes its secret powers of healing:

> Take of English earth as much
> As either hand may rightly clutch.
> In the taking of it breathe
> Prayer for all who lie beneath.
> Not the great nor well-bespoke,
> But the mere uncounted folk
> Of whose life and death is none
> Report or lamentation.
> Lay that earth upon thy heart
> And thy sickness shall depart.

What fervour in these final lines! what a sense of peace recovered! A balm seems to have been laid upon this heart, which drinks it in with silent passion.

> It shall sweeten and make whole
> Fevered breath and festered soul,
> It shall mightily restrain
> Over-busied hand and brain.
> It shall ease thy mortal strife
> 'Gainst the immortal woe of life.

Which of us has not felt the sweetness of coming back to one's own soil? We feel ourselves enfolded, recaptured; it is like an old nurse's song murmuring in our ears again ; we pause and half close our eyes to listen. . . . .

But the song here dates from further back than childhood—from the bygone times of all those dead whose ashes, mingled with this soil, give it its healing virtue. They have left their traces everywhere : in the old lanes barred by gates that have always been there, in the manor-house with its smoke curling up behind the wood, in the trees on the village green, in the low Norman church watching over the tombstones on which eighteenth-century dates are still visible.

And if one stays long enough in the country and learns to read the writing of time upon it, other traces reveal themselves, and gradually the most distant past appears :

> See you the ferny ride that steals
>   Into the oak-woods far ?
> O that was whence they hewed the keels
>   That rolled to Trafalgar !
>
> See you the dimpled track that runs
>   All hollow through the wheat ?
> O that was where they hauled the guns
>   That smote King Philip's fleet !
>
> See you our stilly woods of oak
>   And the dread ditch beside ?
> O that was where the Saxons broke
>   On the day that Harold died.

Thus from age to age the life of the Sussex Weald is conjured up, back to the dawn of History, when the English land was Britain, back to that night without a beginning which preceded History. Some mounds in

the soil, the vestige of a moat to be seen only after
rain : it is the camp of a Roman legion, when Cæsar
had crossed the seas. And fainter still, those long
lines, like shadows on the downs where sheep-bells
tinkle, mark a fortification made by men of the Flint
Age :

> Trackway and Camp and City lost,
> Salt marsh where now is corn,
> Old Wars, old Peace, old Arts that cease
> And so was England born.
>
> She is not any common earth
> Water, or wood or air,
> But Merlin's Isle of Gramarye
> Where you and I will fare.[1]

How these words open up the dream-vista ! The
mystery of a long tide of life that has brought millions
of human forms—and nothing of them remains but the
onward movement within ourselves ! The mystery of
what has been, is no more, and yet continues in our
present, that elusive present, ever vanishing—unless it
alone be the one ever-enduring moment ! The mystery
of those generations from whom we come, who lived a
hundred, a thousand years ago, on the very place
where we now stand, on this soil of clay or chalk,
among these same fields and streams, and were like
us—and they have passed away, and we pass in our
turn, and these hills behold the procession of forms
ever repeated. Carlyle, too, had this vision of mankind
appearing in Time and expanding between two voids
like a rainbow projected by a motionless sun. It

[1] *Puck's Song* in *Puck of Pook's Hill.*

filled him with amazement to say to himself, to realise
with his mind's eye that a John Lackland had actually
been *there*, that the England of 1200, of which a Dryas-
dust makes an abstraction, was a solid green land
where corn and other things grew, where the sun
shone, where men wove and ploughed, and men and
cattle rose at morn to work, and returned at night
to their homes. Kipling shows us the same view,
reversed. Looking round his familiar landscape, he
marvels to think that the men and things of to-day are
the same as those of distant ages, that the small voice
of the stream was singing in the twelfth century in this
very dell, that old man Hobden, who clips the squire's
hedge, comes from a Hobden who in those far-away
days clipped the hedge of a knight—that before
him there were others of the name, who lived by the
same bread, the same beliefs and customs, in the same
circle of the horizon. Thus, in the souls of the men as
in the soil of the countryside the past persists. " What
has been will be," says the great lonely serpent of the
jungle, who has lived a thousand years. And when
he awakes from his long torpors he cannot tell whether
the living round him are or are not those he has known.

This haunting vision of a past, everywhere traced
in the present, has sent Kipling to History, and gives
deep poetry to his reconstructions. In a series of tales
and songs in which Puck, who has seen the tide of
human generations flowing through the Island, tells of
its memories and secrets, and lends the author his
magic, the latter conjures up some of the figures which
passed through the land in the course of centuries—

smugglers of the time of Pitt and the French Revolution, squires of the eighteenth century, gentlemen of
Queen Bess's day, artisans of the reign of Henry VII.,
Jews and Barons of the Middle Ages, comrades of the
Conqueror, Saxon thanes, worshippers of the Northern
gods, whose names still linger in those of certain springs
and fords, legionaries who sang the hymns of Mithra,
Romans (sons of Roman officials born in Cambria, just
as in our own days a certain English singer, the son of
an English civil servant, was born in the Punjaub),
officers of Cæsar, who defended the passes of Caledonia
against the Picts, and held the same idea of Empire
and service as the King's officers of to-day who keep a
pass of the Himalayas against the Afghans. For what
has been, is, and the living repeat the dead.

Long quotations would be required to give an idea
of the accurate and profuse detail which lends reality
to these phantoms of the past. Here the writer shows
the same strange power of rediscovering and recreating
the dead Past as the hero in *The Finest Story in the
World*. But this power is not mere divination. It is
rather a kind of insight. An object is noted and penetrated more quickly and deeply than with ordinary
eyes. With the same fervour, the same swift perception
that had served him to seize upon the essential facts
and aspects of the living world, he has considered the
monuments and traces of the past and sought out their
meaning. He has read the texts, has become an his-
torian, collaborating in a *History of England* for the
young, and here again he has scattered verse between
the chapters, revealing in their music the hidden sense

of history, the deep, directing ideas, the tendency which events have gradually realised : the age-long growth, through checks and adverse seasons, knot on knot, ring on ring, of that oak which has borne the English generations, and whose branches now cover so great a space on the globe.

Thus it is that the sense of Country has gone on deepening in Kipling. He was at first in love with the strength and beauty of the foliage ; later on, he noted more especially the ancient life of the trunk ; he was moved by the sight of the marks of time, of the deep strata whereon each development, each age has been imprinted. The time was far distant when he had sung : " What do they know of England who only England know ? " No longer a traveller, attached henceforth to the old soil, where so many men of his race had been rooted, behind the living he saw the dead, those dead who had not dreamt of the Empire, but had prepared it by their virtues, and he loved the land where their traces are everywhere to be seen, loved it simply, as they had loved it. " The land and its dead," as we say in France. His patriotism is no longer proud and exultant as in his youth ; it has become more inward and tender, more like our own ; it is tinged with a feeling akin to that suggested in the French saying— a feeling which, as early as the eleventh century, had found expression in the words : *Douce France*.

But the earlier vision persists, it has only become deeper. It now embraces the whole life of the English hive. The conception of present society as formed by the living who owe service to one another and to future generations, has been completed by that of the bond between these living and all the generations before them. Not that Kipling was ever unmindful of the dead—they have their *Saga* in *The Song of the English*. But in this he sings only of the pioneers of new Englands, those whose bones lie rotting at the bottom of the sea, or strew the first trails in Veldt and Prairie, not of all those millions whose dust, mingled with English earth for a thousand years, makes it holy to an English heart.

Does this mean that his love of country is greater now than of old ? But is complete knowledge necessary to love ? Is it not rather because one *loves* that one longs to know better and better—to know those hidden things of the soul, those dim recesses of the past undiscerned by a young poet, face to face with the beauty that first moves him to sing ? Kipling's patriotism was the passion that shaped his life. It proclaimed itself ingenuously in his first poem, written at the age of sixteen ; it inspires the stanzas dated on the eve of the Armistice. An ever-present, restless passion—an active passion which has set him apart, consecrated him, and marked him with a sign.

What the approach, and finally, the outbreak of the Great War was to a mind thus possessed, we can now conceive. Better than any other his special and highly trained sensibility had prepared him to react to the tremendous event and see it, I do not say in itself, in all its foreign origins, but from the national point of view, as a deathly shadow ever denser, about to pass over England. On the English retina, made up of millions of sensitive cells, his mind was, so to speak, the point where the image reaches its highest degree of truth and precision.

Of this dread image so few of us had conceived until it actually confronted us, we may see the birth in Kipling's mind some twenty years before. We may see it assuming a definite form and becoming more and more charged with emotion. We may follow its haunting growth in his lyric work, from suspicion to passionate conviction, and finally, to immediate visionary certainty. Then it was that he began to denounce the sins of his people, to point out the danger and interpret signs and tokens. And his tone was enough : before the predictions were fulfilled, the prophet had already appeared in the poet.

VI.—THE PROPHECY OF WAR

It was indeed the watchfulness and divination of Love.

Already, in 1890, he had spoken of the great test which would decide the fate of the English. We have seen how this anxious prescience led him to preach the idea of Empire, to urge the union of the sister nations

" In the day of Armageddon, at the last great fight of all,
That our House stand together and the pillars do not fall."

Nowadays this word Armageddon, which was on all English lips during the war, has a more actual and tragic sense than when Kipling wrote it first. Had he Germany in his mind at the time? A poem of the same year did indeed give utterance to his distrust of the young Kaiser, whose scheme of international legislation for Labour seemed to him aimed at English industry.[1] But more probably he was thinking of Russia, who in 1890 was believed to be threatening India and all Western Europe—we saw that he learned Russian at school in order to keep watch against this danger, and that later, it was his business to study the *Novoe Vremya* in 1885 in the offices of the *Pioneer*. In any case, he argued that youthful hungry nations were growing up on all sides, that some day surely the glove would be thrown down to an aged England, the mistress of so much wealth and territory acquired in less strenuous times.

Twelve years later, immediately after the South African War, he wrote *The Rowers*, where he boldly points out, and all but names, the formidable, hate-ridden enemy, and this with a resentment, a contempt, that sufficiently expresses his opinion of Germany, of her designs and methods. Those who were in favour of accepting the German proposal of an Anglo-German expedition to Venezuela he denounced as men who had made a secret pact with an "open foe," with "the breed that has wronged us most," "the Goth and the shameless Hun." The Kaiser had just issued his famous proclamation proposing the hordes of Attila as models to his troops in China. Thus, the poet who had foretold Armageddon in 1890, in 1902 denounced

[1] *An Imperial Rescript.*

the German as the Hun. These two terms, adopted by all England, became the *Leitmotiv* of the Great War.

In the interval his suspicions had become rooted. In 1896 he had felt not only the insult, but the political intention of the Imperial telegram to President Kruger. At Cologne in the following year the Kaiser had declared that the trident must be in Germany's hand; at Stettin in 1898, that the future of Germany was on the sea. The first naval programme coincided with this speech; in 1900 it was brought forward again, but with enormous additions, and there was an outburst of Anglophobia throughout the Reich, instigated by a disciplined press. The great idea of the reign now began to be seen: Germany's second advance, the extension to the world of the hegemony established by the first William in Europe. Such a development was bringing Germany up against every English position on the globe. The Transvaal affair raised in her hopes of support in the trial of strength. Were there not hopes of such support even from the West?

At that time a personal experience helped to awaken Kipling's instinctive sense of the enemy. In 1898 he was in Pretoria, where German officers were superintending the mounting of heavy Krupp guns on the forts of the town. Here it was that he made acquaintance with blue uniform and spiked helmet, with the haughty stare of the monocle, the swaggering tread of heavy boot and spurred heel, the clank of trailing scabbards, the insolent elbowing that hustled an Englishman off the footpath. Such an experience was an enduring

memory to an intuitive poet, who had proudly sung
of the British Empire.

Henceforth, in his more important poems, the
warning note sounds continually. The whole Prelude
to *The Five Nations* (1903) is a startling prediction—
written, probably, after all the other verse in the
volume. Thinking of the many signs a blind England
had failed to mark, the poet enumerates them in a
series of Sibylline images :

> Before a midnight breaks in storm
>   Or herded sea in wrath,
> Ye know what wavering gusts inform
>   The greater tempest's path ;
>   Till the loosed wind
>   Drive all from mind
> Except Distress, which, so will prophets cry,
> O'ercame them, houseless, from the unhinting sky.
>
> Ere rivers league against the land
>   In piratry of flood,
> Ye know what waters slip and stand
>   Where seldom water stood
>   Yet who will note,
>   Till fields afloat,
> And washen carcass and the return.
> Trumpet what these poor heralds strove to te.. .

Other images follow : the Crystal Ball used " to peer
by stealth on Doom," the Shade that passes " like
breath from glass." And then the warning of the days
when men, aghast, shall see the pregnant Earth " bow
to the birth and sweat " to bring forth Disaster, before
the sport-making Gods, " like Samson, slaying, die."
And finally, the appeal to the " winged men the Fates
may breed, so soon as Fate hath wings " :

RUDYARD KIPLING

>These shall possess
>Our littleness
>And in the imperial task (as worthy) lay
>Up our lives' all to piece one giant day.

What fulness and certitude of vision in these dedi-
catory lines! Here was no chance perception, no
inspiration of a moment. In language less oracular,
more human, but still symbolical, ten poems, the
greatest and most intense in this collection, which
contains but forty, show us different aspects of the same
idea. *The Bell-Buoy* (1896), one of the finest and most
purely poetic, setting forth the poet's own mission—not,
after the manner of others, to sing, and delight men
like the sweet bells of minster-towers, but to ride on
the surf of tempests crying aloud the hidden danger.
Perhaps also the poem called *The Old Issue* (1899),
where part of the allusion seems to be to Germany, to
the prince who sets himself " above the Law, calling on
the Lord," and to his captains, who " jeer us in the
street." And undoubtedly, the whole of the 1902
series, stern objurgations to a lethargic England in
peril.

The first of these is *The Dykes*, where the poet sings
of the defences raised by watchful forefathers. Too
long have their sons, safe behind the dykes, far from the
beach, forgotten the sea and neglected the outworks.
And the sea is rising, the flood-tide rushes on in the
darkness, lashed by the storm, turning and returning
the shingle, baying along the wall, mounting to the
crest of the dyke. Again and again have there been
signs of foul weather, fitful rays that vanish and

return, evil embers bedded in ash, sparks blown west
by the wind ; now " we are surrendered to night and
the sea—the gale and the tide behind ! "

Ninefold deep to the top of the dykes the galloping
    breakers stride,
And their over-carried spray is a sea—a sea on the
    landward side.
Coming, like stallions they paw with their hooves,
    going they snatch with their teeth,
Till the bents and the furze and the sand are dragged
    out, and the old-time wattles beneath.

Bid men gather fuel for fire, the tar and the oil and the
    tow—
Flame we shall need, not smoke in the dark if the
    riddled sea-banks go.
Bid the ringers watch in the tower (who knows what the
    dawn shall prove ?)
Each with his rope between his feet and the trembling
    bells above.

Now we can only wait till the day, wait and apportion
    our shame,
These are the dykes our fathers left, but we would not
    look to the same.
Time and again were we warned of the dykes, time and
    again we delayed :
Now it may fall we have slain our sons as our fathers
    we have betrayed.

Walking along the wreck of the dykes, watching the
    work of the seas,
These were the dykes our fathers made to our great
    profit and ease ;
But the peace is gone, and the profit is gone, and the
    old sure days withdrawn . . .
That our own houses show as strange when we come
    back in the dawn !

RUDYARD KIPLING

The war was to make plain, not the idea of these verses—that was evident—but the significance of certain images, and the burning emotion they express. Eleven years before the first gun was fired, Kipling, foreseeing a sensation no one else could imagine, realised what our feeling was to be at the end of August, 1914, when the Germans were within ten leagues of Paris, and we were waiting for the first shells to fall. Then, indeed, when we looked at our gray Parisian houses, six or seven storeys high, which might all crash down the next day, it seemed to us—strangely—as if we saw them for the first time. Familiar things, all our world around us, took on a new aspect, when we realised that this, our French world, so difficult to think of from without, because it is the very foundation of our being, might presently be swallowed up in flame and thunder. Another image is no less poignant, and the presentiment that inspired it was so strong that it broke out almost in a cry of anguish : " Now it may fall we have slain our sons ! " What words on the lips of a father whose son Fate had already marked.

The " we " here is that England which refuses to open her eyes, to leave her games, her business, her intestine quarrels, to prepare her defences and weapons, and show her strength, the mere sight of which, as we know now, as the poet knew fifteen years ago, would have averted the catastrophe. This is the idea which recurs in the other great poems of 1902—*The Lesson, The Old Men, The Reformers, The Islanders*—with all the concentrated passion and inspired certitude we have already noted. The Lesson then to be laid to heart was that of the Transvaal War : the Old Men are those who " assume they are alive, whereas they are really dead . . ." who " will not acknowledge that old stars fade or alien planets arise " ; the Reformers, on the other hand, are those who see realities, " the imperishable plinth of things seen and unseen that touch our peace," those who do not place the word above the fact, who turn away from the idols of their nation, accepting and proclaiming necessities. The Islanders are the people who can see no further than their island, who live in illusions, who believe the lies of their shepherds, who refuse a year of service to their country—a country whose life has been so long untroubled that they imagine it to be eternal as the mountains : but

It was not made with the mountains, it is not one with
    the deep.
Men, not gods, devised it, men, not gods, must keep.
Men, not children, servants, or kinsfolk called from afar,
But each man born in the Island broke to the matter of
    war.
So ye shall bide sure-guarded when the restless lightnings
    wake
In the womb of the blotting war-cloud, and the pallid
    nations quake.
So at the haggard trumpets instant your soul shall
    leap
Forthright, accoutred, accepting—alert from the wells
    of sleep.
But ye say, " It will mar our comfort." Ye say, " It
    will minish our trade."
Do ye wait for the spattered shrapnel ere ye learn how
    a gun is laid ?

RUDYARD KIPLING

For the low red glare to southward when the raided
    coast towns burn ?
(Light ye shall have on that lesson, but little time to
    learn.)
Will the rabbit war with your foemen ?—the red deer
    horn them for hire,
Your kept cock-pheasant keep you ?—he is master of
    many a shire.
Arid, aloof, incurious, unthinking, unthanking, gelt,
Will ye loose your schools to flout them till their brow-
    beat columns melt ?
Will ye pray them or preach them or print them, or
    ballot them back from your shore?
Will your workmen issue a mandate to bid them strike
    no more ?
Will ye rise and dethrone your rulers ?   (Because ye
    were idle both ?
Pride by insolence chastened ?   Indolence purged by
    sloth ?)
No doubt but ye are the People—absolute, strong and
    wise ;
Whatever your heart has desired ye have not withheld
    from your eyes,
On your own heads, in your own hands, the sin and the
    saving lies !

    Englishmen who read these poems to-day may be
moved by them. In 1902, urgent as was the warning,
John Bull, when he found them in his *Times,* as he
sat down to his morning tea and eggs, passed on from
them to the sporting and Stock Exchange news. The
Transvaal business was over ; at last one could forget
the war. This Kipling, prophesying slaughter with
his Isaiah attitude, had a queer way of celebrating
victory. And, indeed, he was lashing at the whole
English nation, every class and every party ; the

middle classes, intent on their shops and business; the gentry and aristocracy, thinking only of their sport and week-ends; the workmen, absorbed in their football bets and their unions; the Tories, the Liberals, Labour—for Right and Left, all parliamentary groups alike were unanimous in refusing the one measure which to the poet meant salvation.

But when the struggle between Right and Left grew keener, especially after the elections of 1906, which brought the Radicals into power, the latter gradually emerged as the chief opponents, not of a scheme of compulsory military service—no such project was ever submitted to Parliament—but of any attempt to prepare the country for danger, and indeed of the very suggestion of danger: the idea was considered antagonistic to democratic thought, then setting in the direction of sweeping popular reforms. For if there were really danger to be faced, reform would have to take the very opposite direction; it would mean, not the reign of the masses, but a general submission to authority and competence; not the prosperity and equality of all, but discipline, renunciation and effort; not more rights, but more duties. Men would have to abandon party warfare and prepare for national warfare, to organise on military lines for efficient and continuous action. This was why the Radicals, from their chief downwards, passionately denied the existence of peril. A Tory invention, clamoured their journalists, orators, canvassers, candidates, during the elections of 1910; a device to hamper democratic progress. Nor were the Radicals content merely to deny danger, and to fight against the ideas of which Kipling, taking his stand beside old Field-Marshal Roberts, was the champion ; they dreamed of reducing armaments, and in fact, did reduce them. From 1905 to 1909, when Germany increased her naval estimates by 162 millions of marks, England reduced hers by 7 million pounds.[1]

Thenceforth, the poet looked upon Radicalism as the enemy within, preparing the way for the foe without, disintegrating England by class war, blinding her to the evidence of peril, paralysing her reactions and atrophying her organs of defence prior to handing her over helpless to the enemy. It was Kipling's patriotism that impelled him to denounce democracy. Scathing are the accusations implied in the images of *The City of Brass*, the story of a people, or rather of *the* People, Demos, whose folly has hurled them into the abyss.

They rose to suppose themselves kings over all things created—
To decree a new earth at a birth without labour or sorrow—
To declare : " We prepare it to-day and inherit to-morrow."
They chose themselves prophets and priests of minute understanding,

[1] The same tendency persisted on the very eve of the war. On January 1st, 1914, Mr. Lloyd George declared, in an interview reported by the *Daily Chronicle*, that the moment was favourable to a revision of the Budget for armament, as relations with Germany were more friendly than they had been for some time. And on July 23rd, the very date of Austria's ultimatum to Serbia, he rebuked Mr. Austen Chamberlain for supposing that military expenses would continue.

Then swift to see done, and outrun, their extremest
    commanding—
Of the tribe which describe with a jibe the perversions
    of Justice,
Panders avowed to the crowd whatever its lust is.

Swiftly these pulled down the walls that their fathers
    had made them,
The impregnable ramparts of old, they razed and relaid
    them
As playgrounds of pleasure and leisure with limitless
    entries,
And havens of rest for the wastrels where once walked
    the sentries.
And because there was need of more pay for the shouters
    and marchers,
They disbanded in face of the foemen their bowmen and
    archers.
They replied to their well-wishers' fear—to their
    enemies' laughter,
Saying " Peace. We have fashioned a God which shall
    save us hereafter.
We ascribe all dominion to man in his factions
    conferring,
And have given to numbers the name of the Wisdom
    unerring."
They said : " Who has hate in his soul ? Who has
    envied his neighbour ?
Let him arise and control both that man and his
    labour."
They said : " Who is eaten by sloth ? Whose unthrift
    has destroyed him ?
He shall levy a tribute from all because none have
    employed him."

And the men of this city have not only destroyed
their material defences :

RUDYARD KIPLING

They ran panting in haste to lay waste and embitter
   for ever
The wellsprings of Wisdom and Strength which are
   Faith and Endeavour.
They nosed out and digged up, and dragged forth and
   exposed to derision
All doctrine of purpose and worth and restraint and
   prevision.

   .   .   .   .   .

When they were fullest of wine and most flagrant in
   error,
Out of the sea rose a sign—out of Heaven a terror.
Then they saw, then they heard, then they knew, for
   none troubled to hide it,
An host had prepared their destruction, but still they
   denied it.
They denied what they dared not abide if it came to the
   trial,
But the Sword that was forged while they lied did not
   heed their denial.
It drove home, and no time was allowed to the crowd
   that was driven.
There was no need of a steed nor a lance to pursue
   them ;
It was decreed their own deed and not chance should
   undo them.
The tares they had laughingly sown were ripe to the
   reaping. . . .
The hate they had taught through the State brought
   the State no defender,
And it passed from the roll of the nations in headlong
   surrender.

   This was one of Kipling's solemn warnings, then
deeply resented by many. We soon forget : when
his countrymen read these verses to-day, do they
remember the anguish of every British heart in August,

1914, after Mons ; in April, 1917, when the submarine peril was revealed in all its terror ; in March 1918, when the German advance threatened to sweep forward to the Channel ? On each of these dates the fate of England trembled in the balance.

In 1909, about the time when Kipling made this appeal, the coming struggle was so evident to him that he said to a Frenchman, who here testifies to the fact : " The one thing you and we have to think of now is war." He himself was thinking of it so much, that he accompanied Lord Roberts in his visits to France to arrange for possible military co-operation of the two countries, should German aggression change the *Entente* into an alliance. He himself began to work for such an alliance, and in his short *History of England* (1911), where he speaks of the north-east wind which has always been an ill wind for Great Britain, the idea inspired his stirring songs on the old heroic quarrels of the two peoples.

For now the mutterings of the German thunder were waxing louder—first the Bosnia-Herzegovina business, then the Kaiser's shining armour speech, and the affair of the Casablanca deserters ; then the Agadir incident with the explosion of *furor teutonicus* that followed on the intervention of England. Insults were thrown at her ; a campaign against Sir Edward Grey was started, in the hope of driving him from office, as M. Delcassé had been driven in 1905. Against France the theory of France as a " hostage nation " was invented ; a murder-policy was avowed, some newspapers advocating a war of extermination and suggest-

ing the flooding of the coal-pits, the destruction of the
wealth of France for fifty years. In February, 1912,
Lord Haldane undertook his useless but illuminating
mission to Berlin ; new credits for the army and navy
were voted in the Reichstag ; in April there was a
fresh naval programme, and in the following year
another and still more formidable naval budget. Thus
was gradually unfolded that " will to power " which
from 1896 onwards, had been working towards its ends
with a logic and a patience that almost compel admiration. Sensational as the final developments were, they
failed to rouse English public opinion, carefully lulled
to sleep by the Kaiser's visits (1902–1907), by the
corporate visits of professors, pastors, burgomasters,
merchants, and the untiring efforts of Germany's
agents.

But there were some who had never ceased to watch
and to warn, and these knew that the eleventh hour
had come. In this last year of the peace of the world,
Kipling no longer addressed himself to England, but
to France. For the time of long party debates upon
military laws and armaments was past. In 1913 one
thing was more important than all the rest : the
alliance ; the two peoples must know that they stood
together. Nor was it only their need that was to unite
them. In the face of a menacing new nation, he urges
them to remember the thousand years they have lived
side by side, and what each of the two neighbours owes
to the other of her history, civilisation and destiny.
This idea was no invention of the poet. It was born
and took shape long before the war, as the British

became conscious of the keen rivalry and ill-will of the Germans. Twenty years ago I heard it expressed in reference to the attitude of the French during the South African War. "We were more sensitive to this," I was told by English friends, "than to all the noisy German Anglophobia. We value French opinion more than any other. We have lived in close communion with you for so long, with you alone among the nations. The very memory of our old battles unites us." Such was the theme of the poem that Kipling entitled *France* :

Ere our birth (rememberest thou ?) side by side we lay
Fretting in the womb of Rome to begin our fray.
Ere men knew our tongues apart, our one task was
    known—
Each must mould the other's fate as he wrought his
    own.
To this end we stirred mankind till all Earth was ours,
Till our world end strifes begat wayside thrones and
    powers. . . .
To this end we stormed the seas, tack for tack, and
    burst
Through the doorways of new worlds, doubtful which
    was first.
Hand on hilt (rememberest thou ?) ready for the blow—
Sure, whatever else we met, we should meet our foe.
Spurred or balked at every stride by the other's
    strength,
So we rode the ages down and every ocean's length. . . .
Each the other's mystery, terror, need and love.
To each other's open court with our proofs we came.
Where could we find honour else, or men to test our
    claim ?
From each other's throat we wrenched—valour's last
    reward—

That extorted word of praise gasped 'twixt lunge and
    guard.
In each other's cup we poured mingled blood and tears,
Brutal joys, unmeasured hopes, intolerable fears—
All that soiled or salted life for a thousand years.
Proved beyond the need of proof, matched in every
    clime,
O companion, we have lived greatly through all time !

Yoked in knowledge and remorse now we come to rest.
Laughing at old villainies that Time has turned to jest ;
Pardoning old necessities no pardon can efface—
That undying sin we shared in Rouen market-place.
Now we watch the new years shape, wondering if they
    hold
Fiercer lightnings in their heart than we launched of
    old.
Now we hear new voices rise, question, boast, or
    gird . . .
Now we count new keels afloat, and new hosts on
    land . . .
Listen, count and close again, wheeling girth to girth
In the linked and stedfast guard set for peace on earth.

This last image is a vivid rendering of a then popular
idea : England and France as the two knightly nations
of Europe, noble by virtue of their age and their
ancient prowess, in contrast to the newcomers, and
now the champions of the moral and liberal civilisation
of the West, of which they were the pioneers. Among
all the imponderables which moved so many Englishmen to take their stand for honour's sake beside France
in July, 1914, even before the decisive violation of
Belgian neutrality, the influence of these grand verses
may perhaps be reckoned.

ENGLISH LITERATURE

VII.—THE WAR POEMS

At last the sands have run out and the prophecies are fulfilled. The Day has come—" the Day, the giant Day," solemnly announced in 1903—that Armageddon —foretold in 1890, the thought of which had run through Kipling's whole life, and coloured all his poetry. When that pale dawn arose, so soon to be dyed blood-red, and two nations prepared to defend their lives, their souls, and the heritage of a thousand years, a kind of hush fell on the world. The statesmen were silent. From one end of Europe to the other nothing was heard but the tramp of marching legions. In France, the country most directly threatened, whence the foreigner expected cries and burning words, not even the *Marseillaise* was heard. And when a voice was raised in England, the voice that had spoken at all the great moments of the country's history for nearly twenty-five years, how simple, stern, almost cold it sounded in its Puritan austerity ! It was the tone of prayer and exhortation, when the priest speaks alone above the awed silence of a congregation, in the bare choir of an Anglican church.

> For all we have and are,
> For all our children's fate,
> Stand up and take the war,
> The Hun is at the gate.
> Our world has passed away,
> In wantonness o'erthrown.
> There is nothing left to-day
> But steel and fire and stone !

Though all we knew depart,
The old Commandments stand—
" In courage keep your heart,
In strength lift up your hand."

.   .   .

Comfort, content, delight,
The ages' slow-bought gain,
They shrivelled in a night.
Only ourselves remain
To face the naked days
In silent fortitude,
Through perils and dismays
Renewed and re-renewed.
Though all we made depart,
The old Commandments stand—
" In patience keep your heart,
In strength lift up your hand."

No easy hope or lies
Shall bring us to our goal,
But iron sacrifice
Of body, will and soul.
There is but one task for all—
One life for each to give.
Who stands if Freedom fall ?
Who dies if England live ?

Such is the tense and rigorous accent of this war-
poetry, asserting the immutability of conscience, the
strength and tenacity of the will it upholds. Not only
the patriotism, but the religion of a people is here
expressed, their faith in the Commandments and in
eternal distinction between right and wrong. Theirs
was the task to prevent that upheaval and confusion of
the moral universe which would follow the reign of
crime on earth, to maintain the law against those who

had broken it—*the Outlaws*, as the poets call them, the men who " through learned and laborious years had set themselves to find fresh terrors to heap upon mankind " ; who had " plotted by their neighbours' hearth the means to make him slave " ; those who had " laid waste a land their oath was pledged to guard," and had marched towards their goal across a world in flame—but their souls had been slain by their own hate.

For in such warfare a nation saves or loses her soul. And when the spiritual destiny of the world is at stake, a nation may lose her soul by refusing to take part in it, or even to speak the word that would help the cause of Right. This is the contention in the stern poem of 1916, called *The Question*, addressed to the people of like culture, ideals, religion, to the kindred people who were finally to draw the sword, but who so far had uttered no protest against the crime.

> Brethren, how shall it fare with me
> When the war is laid aside,
> If it be proved that I am he
> For whom a world has died ?
>
> That I was delivered by mere mankind
> Vowed to one sacrifice,
> And not, as I hold them, battle-blind,
> But dying with open eyes ?
>
> That they did not ask me to draw the sword
> When they stood to endure their lot—
> That they only looked to me for a word,
> And I answered I knew them not ?
>
> If it be found when the battle clears
> Their death has set me free,
> Then how shall I live with myself through the years
> Which they have bought for me ?

RUDYARD KIPLING

That was the question : the answer came in 1917.
The poet might have been expected to celebrate by
some lyrical outburst the crusader zeal of those who
had so long hesitated. But even then he sounds the
same note of tense, stark fervour :

> Not at a little cost,
> Hardly by prayer or tears,
> Shall we recover the road we lost
> In the drugged and doubting years.
>
> But after the fires and the wrath,
> But after searching and pain,
> His Mercy opens us a path
> To live with ourselves again.
>
> Then praise the Lord most High
> Whose strength hath saved us whole,
> Who bade us choose that the flesh should die
> And not the living soul !

He alone who so long and so anxiously had seen the
war coming could have spoken thus. And having
thought of it for thirty years more deeply perhaps than
any in his country, he could note from hour to hour all
the pity and horror of it, and also all the exaltation.
At critical moments his underlying stoicism reappears,
but how far he is from assuming the rigid attitude of
the high priest ! If, more quickly than others, he
responds to all the drama of the war, it is in the midst
of others—others who are suffering, hoping, despairing,
weeping, and at times laughing, too. " For as we live
and as we die," he had declared, " the people, Lord,
Thy people, are good enough for me." His theme is
suffering, but nevertheless, with all the rest, with all

129

who go forth to fight by land or sea, he can sing and
laugh. He sings with the Irish, " who move to the
sound of the guns like salmon to the sea," and all the
music, all the dancing fancy of Erin is in the refrain,
with its love of battle and love of France, the refrain
of the Irish Guards, who once fared through France in
scarlet coats, " carrying their packs with Marshal Saxe
when Louis was their King."

> *But Douglas Haig's our Marshal now*
> *And we're King George's men,*
> *And after one hundred and seventy years*
> *We're fighting for France again !*
> *Ah, France ! and did we stand by you,*
> *When life was made splendid with gifts and rewards ?*
> *Ah, France ! And will we deny you*
> *In the hour of your agony, Mother of Swords ?*
> *Old Days ! The wild geese are flighting,*
> *Head to the storm as they faced it before,*
> *For where there are Irish there's loving and fighting,*
> *And when we stop either, it's Ireland no more.*
> > *Ireland no more.*

A clear, thrilling bugle-call, marking the time and
quickening the movement of the poem.

To appreciate the fulness of the singer's sympathy,
the eagerness with which he followed all the aspects
of the war, we should read the poems that tell of
the patient, strenuous toil, the obscure daily heroism
of humble crews of trawlers and fishing-smacks,
turned into patrol-boats and mine-sweepers in the
North Sea. What a picture of faithfulness and strict
obedience to orders, on the gray waters of that wintry
waste !

Dawn off the Foreland—the young flood making
  Jumbled and short and steep—
Black in the hollows and bright where it's
    breaking—
  Awkward water to sweep.
      " Mines reported in the fairway,
      Warn all traffic and detain.
Sent up *Unity, Claribel, Assyrian, Stormcock and
  Golden Grain.*"

Noon off the Foreland—the first ebb making
  Lumpy and strong in the bight
Boom after boom, and the golf-hut shaking
  And the jackdaws wild with fright !
      " Mines located in the fairway,
      Boats now working up the chain,
Sweepers—*Unity, Claribel, Assyrian, Stormcock* and
  Golden Grain."

Dusk off the Foreland—the last light going
  And the traffic crowding through,
And five damned trawlers with their syrens blowing
  Heading the whole review !
      " Sweep completed in the fairway,
      No more mines remain.
Sent back *Unity, Claribel, Assyrian, Stormcock* and
  Golden Grain."

How swift and sure the touch of the artist ! All
who know anything of the sea will recognise the life
of the northern waters, the deep, relentless cosmic
force of the tide, a wilder force in those narrow seas that
do not feel the long rhythmic ocean swell, but leap up
directly wind and current are in conflict. And then,
above the swirling waters, the shifting winter lights,
the lurid dawn, the gloomy day, the lingering yellow
twilight, and, steadfast in the welter, the watchful

energy of men at work whose thought invisibly flashes through space.

Other poems are dramatic, instinct with war-passion and the hatred the lawless enemy, slaughtering women and children, had finally taught to the English masses. For instance, the soliloquy of Mrs. Embsay, a war-widow whose son also has been killed by the Germans, and who has been working for two years in a munition factory. Seated at her lathe in the whirr and glitter of steel, she thinks, and her thought works in concert with her hand—a hand that now needs no conscious guidance. She thinks of her dead, of the war and what it means to her, and under these floating visions broken by the sight of realities—long rows of machines, piles of metal—one dark, fixed idea recurs : the guns, the guns, and the shells for which they hunger, which they must have to avenge the dead.

The fans and the beltings they roar round me.
The power is shaking the floor round me
Till the lathes pick up their duty and the midnight
    shift takes over.
        It is good for me to be here.

     Guns in Flanders—Flanders' guns !
     (I had a man that worked 'em once !)
     Shells for guns in Flanders, Flanders !
     Shells for guns in Flanders, Flanders !
       Shells for guns in Flanders ! Feed the guns !

The Zeppelins and Gothas they raid over us.
Our lights give warning, and fade over us.
Seven thousand women keeping quiet in the darkness !
    Oh ! it is good for me to be here !

  .   .   .   .   .

RUDYARD KIPLING

Once I was a woman, but that's by with me.
All I loved and looked for it must die with me.
But the Lord has left me over for a servant of the
    judgment.
        And I serve His judgments here.

Guns in Flanders—Flanders' guns!
(I had a son that worked them once!)
Shells for guns in Flanders! Flanders!
Shells for guns in Flanders! Flanders!
    Shells for guns in Flanders! Feed the guns!

The muffled tones, the threatening intensity of these
words, recurring and reverberating like the distant
rumble of a storm, suggest the cannonade at Ypres and
Nieuport as it was heard continuously on the English
coast.

But deep as is the emotion here, we are still conscious
of the poet's art and his inventive skill. In other
poems art seems to disappear, so direct and inevitable
is the utterance of the soul. No music in these ; we
hear the very accents of grief and anger—grief, not
of one man, but of all those whose sons have fallen ;
anger against those whose sins of omission and com-
mission caused their death. Such is the theme of
the poem called by that now pathetic title : *The
Children.* Perhaps we shall understand the lament
better if we remember that enigmatic story, *They,* in
which, fifteen years earlier, the poet, already a bereaved
father, had called up the laughter and prattle of childish
voices : voices heard in a mysterious house, the only
inmate of which is a blind woman, her face full of
passionate maternal tenderness, to whom these phantom
voices are the one daily reality. But first the reader

should turn to another tale, that which now precedes the poem.[1]

It introduces a party of young cadets, whose fathers we learned to know in the author's first Anglo-Indian tales, and in whom those fathers seem to live again. The rollicking story brims over with laughter and jokes. We feel the depth and freshness of all this joyous vitality and bubbling youth, eager to pour itself out. The boys are like young colts, frisking at dawn in a dewy meadow. Which of them ever had any foreboding of suffering and death, of the fate that awaited them ? From this exuberant, innocent gaiety we pass to the desolation and anger in the poem, a poem written and added to the story five and a half years later :

> These were our children who died for our lands. They were dear in our sight.
> We have only the memory left of their home-treasured sayings and laughter,
> The price of our loss shall be paid to our hands, not another's hereafter.
> Neither the Alien nor Priest shall decide on it. That is our right.
> *But who shall return us our children ?*

> At the hour the Barbarian chose to disclose his pretences,
> And raged against Man, they engaged, on the breasts that they bared for us,
> The first felon stroke of the sword he had long prepared for us—
> Their bodies were all our defence while we wrought our defences.

[1] *The Honours of War*, in *A Diversity of Creatures.*

RUDYARD KIPLING

They bought us anew with their blood, forbearing to
blame us,
Those hours which we had not made good when the
Judgment o'ercame us.
They believed us and perished for it. Our statecraft,
our learning
Delivered them bound to the Pit and alive to the
burning,
Whither they mirthfully hastened as jostling for
honour.
Not since her birth has our Earth seen such worth
loosed upon her !

Nor was their agony brief, or once only imposed on
them.
The wounded, the war-spent, the sick received no
exemption ;
Being cured they returned and endured and achieved
our redemption,
Hopeless themselves of relief, till Death, marvelling,
closed on them.

That flesh we had nursed from the first in all cleanness
was given
To corruption unveiled and assailed by the malice of
Heaven.
By the heart-shaking jests of Decay where it lolled on
the wires
To be blanched or gay-painted by fumes—to be cindered
by fires—
To be senselessly tossed and re-tossed in stale mutilation
From crater to crater. For this we shall take
expiation.
        But who shall return us our children ?

What grief and resentment in this reiterated question !
Deep and mournful as a knell, it answers the strange cry
which visionary prescience had wrung from the poet and

father fifteen years earlier : *Now it may fall we have slain our sons !* Thus the idea that had so long haunted him, the idea he had never ceased to serve, comes back, no longer a suggestion of a possible future, but full of the anguish of the irreparable past. If England had prepared for war, war would have been averted. Nine hundred thousand young Englishmen would not have been sacrificed if the leaders of their people had not refused to see signs so often pointed out, so obvious. For if Kipling has been acclaimed as prophet, he declines the honour ; saying he has merely an aptitude, rarer than he had supposed, for arithmetic—a certain faculty for recognising that two and two are four. And he neither forgives nor submits ; the same reproach and lament re-echo throughout his war-poetry ; we hear it muttering in those heart-rending little poems he calls *Epitaphs.* Here is one, a terrible one, which might serve for all graves :

> If any question why we died
> Tell them, because our fathers lied.

and here are pitiless lines for a statesman's tomb :

> I could not dig, I dared not rob,
> Therefore I lied to please the mob.
> Now all my lies are proved untrue,
> And I must face the men I slew.
> What tale shall save me here among
> Mine angry and defrauded young ?

Now that the holocaust is over, and memories grow faint, we may wonder at the passion of the indictment. It arises from the intensity of the vision : the vision of a poet with an imagination perhaps unparalleled in recent years, who felt the public woe the more keenly because he had foreseen it and dreaded it so long—the vision of the man who was so cruelly stricken by the war he had foretold. Of all those dead, he could not think in terms of statistics. He sees, he shares all the sufferings, agonies, despairs. The *Epitaphs* show with what fervour he felt for each, how clearly he realised all the tragedy.

" EQUALITY OF SACRIFICE."

A. " I was a ' have.' " B. " I was a ' have-not.' "
(*Together*). " What hast thou given which I gave not ? "

A SON.

My son was killed while laughing at some jest. I would
    I knew
What it was, and it might serve me in a time when jests
    are few.

EX-CLERK.

Pity not ! The Army gave
Freedom to a timid slave ;
In which Freedom did he find
Strength of body, will and mind ;
By which strength he came to prove
Mirth, Companionship and Love ;
For which Love to Death he went,
In which Death he lies content.

THE WONDER.

Body and spirit I surrendered whole
To harsh instructors—and received a soul . . .
If mortal man could change me through and through
From all I was—what may the God not do ?

THE COWARD.

I could not look on Death, which being known,
Men led me to him, blindfold and alone.

SHOCK.

My name, my speech, myself I had forgot.
My wife and children came—I knew them not.
I died. My mother followed. At her call
And on her bosom I remembered all.

THE BEGINNER.

On the first hour of my first day
In the front trench I fell.
(Children in boxes at a play
Stand up to watch it well.)

UNKNOWN FEMALE CORPSE.

Headless, lacking foot and hand,
Horrible I come to land.
I beseech all women's sons
Know I was a mother once.

PELICANS IN THE WILDERNESS.

The blown sand heaps on me, that none may learn
Where I am laid, for whom my children grieve.
O wings that beat at dawning, ye return
Out of the desert to your young at eve.

AN ONLY SON.

I have slain none except my mother. She
(Blessing her slayer) died of grief for me.

A mother's grief, the unquenchable anguish of purest
love on earth! There is nothing that this poet of
energy and character has dealt with more pathetically.
In *The Children*, where sorrow is tearless and indignant,
we recognise the tense, sombre tone of a man's lament.

138

In the wailing cry that goes up one Christmas morning
—a cry of pain unmixed with bitterness or reproach—
we hear a mother, a mother desolate and failing at the
thought of her " missing " son.

> *The Babe was laid in the Manger,*
> *Between the gentle kine—*
> *All safe from cold and danger—*
> But it was not so with mine.
>   (With mine ! With mine !)
> " Is it well with the child, is it well ? "
> The waiting Mother prayed.
> For I know not how he fell,
> And I know not where he is laid.
>
> *A Star stood forth in Heaven ;*
> *The watchers ran to see*
> *The sign of the Promise given—*
> " But there comes no sign to me.
>   (To me ! To me !)
>
> " *My* child died in the dark.
> Is it well with the child, is it well ?
> There was none to tend him or mark,
> And I know not how he fell."
>
> *The Cross was raised on high ;*
> *The Mother grieved beside—*
> " But the Mother saw Him die
> And took Him when He died.
>   (He died ! He died !)
>
> Seemly and undefiled
> His burial-place was made—
> Is it well, is it well with the child ?
> For I know not where he is laid."

A heart-rending lamentation, so simple—its sharp
anguish suggested by the repetition of certain words

that echo in this tortured soul. We have heard many chords in Kipling's poetry, but none quite like this. The lines go through us, like the long drawn notes of a fine violin. They have the same purity, the same almost unbearable intensity, in the expression of a grief akin to despair ; the same power of uttering the un-utterable. Yet the last word is not despair. The idea that commanded the sacrifice has survived the sacrifice and finally uplifts the prostrate soul. Each line reiterated the agonising thought : " I know not where they have laid him." But here comes the last :

" But I know for Whom he fell "—
The steadfast Mother smiled.
" Is it well with the child—is it well ?
It is well—it is well with the child ! "

Between these poems and the songs that told of barrack-rooms and hard campaigns in India and on the veldt, what a world !—wide as between the magnificent red troops of the Victorian days and those khaki-clad legions of stern, devoted men, who, at the call of duty, patiently fought in the mud of Flanders and Picardy for England's life and soul. The travail of the spirit from without to within is now accomplished. Except the song of the loyal Irish, for whom the Great War was an heroic adventure, not a passion, there is nothing in these poems that is not of the kingdom within us, a spiritual interpretation, in terms of the English soul and ethics, of the crisis in which the fate of the world was at stake. The old Puritan conception of·Law and Judgment is expressed with more concentrated fervour than ever in these last poems, and hence their tense secret vibration.

Judgment : how often we hear it fall upon the luke-warm, the unworthy, the guilty—on neutrals, on compatriots, on the enemy nation, on the chiefs who perverted her, and then drove her to the premeditated crime ! It is not always uttered, but how clearly we see it hanging, stern and inevitable, over the man, for instance, who had exalted himself above all men, and whom the poet pictures on his miserable death-bed, babbling his Germanic dogma of pride and blood and reiterating his lying excuses. A terrible scene with three independent parts : the dying man, talking and wandering ; the doctors in consultation, to whom he is but " a case " ; and in the intervals an inflexible voice, that of human conscience, recalling the millions of death-agonies for which this dying man has to answer.

> " This is the State above the Law.
> The Law exists for the State alone."
> [" *This is a gland at the back of the jaw,*
> *And an answering lump by the collar-bone.*"]
> Some die shouting in gas or fire ;
> Some die silent, by shell and shot.
> Some die desperate, caught on the wire ;
> Some die suddenly.   This will not.
> " Regis suprema Voluntas lex."
> [" *It will follow the regular course of throats.*"]
> Some die pinned by the broken decks,
> Some die sobbing between the boats.
> " There is neither Evil nor Good in life
> Except as the needs of the State ordain."
> [" *Since it is rather too late for the knife*
> *All we can do is to mask the pain.*"]

" I will dash to pieces who bar my way.
Woe to the traitor !   Woe to the weak."

" The war was forced on me by my foes.
All that I sought was the right to live."
[" *Don't be afraid of a triple dose :*
The pain will neutralise half we give."]

[" *Here are the needles. See that he dies*
While the effects of the drug endure.
What is the question he asks with his eyes ?
Yes, All Highest, to God, be sure."]

No doubt this All Highest, shown here in all the
nudity of the human worm, alone and accursed of men,
may be left to the end here described.   Not so Germany,
a nation whose life endures for generations. In
October, 1918, when the day of reckoning was drawing
near, Kipling demanded strict justice upon the people
who had broken the law and let death loose upon the
world ; that justice of the sword which leaves an
undeniable mark on body and soul ; the justice to
which the criminal must submit when we hold him at
our mercy, and to which no written paper can make
him submit when his anguish is over.

Across a world where all men grieve
And grieving strive the more,
The great days range like tides and leave
Our dead on every shore.
Heavy the load we undergo,
And our own hands prepare
If we have parley with the foe,
The load our sons must bear.

.   .   .   .

142

A people and their King
Through ancient sin grown strong,
Because they feared no reckoning
Would set no bound to wrong ;
But now their hour is past,
And we, who bore it, find
Evil incarnate held at last
To answer to mankind.

For agony and spoil
Of nations beat to dust,
For poisoned air and tortured soil
And cold, commanded lust,
And every secret woe
The shuddering waters saw—
Willed and fulfilled by high and low—
Let them relearn the Law.

That when the dooms are read,
Nor high nor low shall say—
" My haughty or my humble head
Has saved me in this day."
Till, at the end of time
Their remnant shall recall,
Their fathers' old confederate crime
Availed them not at all.

For, says the poet, without such justice " all is vain
since life on earth began, and the spent world will sink
back again into chaos, hopeless of God and Man." [1]

* *

Such words which strengthened the hearts of a
people in their struggle, will fix it in their memories.
Just as the vision of danger possessed Kipling at every
stage of his work before the war, the remembrance of it

[1] *Justice* in *The Years Between.*

143

and the desire to keep it present in the minds of the English is likely to govern his thought and life henceforth. The image he had seen projected into the future and which had inspired his prophetic poems will not fade. Nay, it seems that it will haunt him, lurid with the horror of experienced realities—past indeed, but affecting his vital feeling of the future, for the danger of yesterday would become the danger of to-morrow could the victors forget. To work against forgetfulness we can reckon on the poet whose foresight, watchfulness, devotion to his life service have been fully proved. The man who thinks with Cecil Rhodes that the English lack imagination, and was but little surprised at their indifference to his warnings, counted a good deal on the tenacity of their memory. He thought that the massive, reticent and dogged people whose dumb virtues he had sung, and whose dangerous slowness he had denounced, would retain impressions driven into their flesh 'by fire and sword—and the better because these had taken time to get home. He believed that the lesson of hate his countrymen had at last learnt under the insults and felon blows of the enemy would endure " through the dull years ahead," and that time would be counted from the day " when the English began to hate." [1]

Perhaps, but this is not very sure. For in a general way we may wonder whether the English mind we have known, and which Kipling and his predecessors have defined, is not undergoing deep change. In days when even species are held mutable, and the atom disinte-

[1] *The Beginnings*, a poem, in *A Diversity of Creatures.*

grates, we may feel doubtful as to the permanence of types not even of the ethnic order. By virtue of an established state of adaptation, a people may preserve its main features for centuries, but should the moral and physical conditions of life change, these may vary, especially if some violent shock precipitate the rupture of forms which often endured only because they happened to be there. National characteristics do not seem to correspond to anything irreducible in men. Simply in a given community certain traits develop and prevail; and through the action of individuals one upon the other, of each generation upon the next, they endure so long that they appear to be organically fixed. But an experiment such as that going on in the United States shows the plasticity of man, and how rapidly he crystallises anew and changes his type when, escaping from his native surroundings, he comes under the influences of a new environment.

And, again, what we take to be an invariable characteristic, latent or manifest in every individual of a people, is often but that of a class or type predominant in the social and political life of the country, therefore conspicuous, and accounted representative. The recent advance of democracy has brought to light a new England, heralded at the general election of 1918 by the presence of eight million electors who had never voted. This England, that of miners, syndicates, Labour (and we should not forget that new element, women voters), does not seem to be of the type which yesterday, and for so long before, had been accounted essentially and immutably English. This type, of aristocratic and rural origin, was formerly personified in the sturdy, stubborn figure of a squire or farmer. It had been kept more or less alive by virtue of its prestige—a prestige to which the ideals of the public school testify. Prepared by a hundred years of intensive urban and industrial life, the type a long democratic travail has brought to birth, and the emergence of which was hastened by the upheaval of the war, may prove more ardent and gregarious, more feminine and unstable.

Among the spiritual traits of the type that seems to be passing away, and which Kipling still considers peculiarly English, some may be attributed to the prolonged action of a certain religious culture. Not in vain can a people have practised for three hundred years that variety of Christianity which insists so much on the threat of eternal punishment, and teaches that each soul stands alone before its God, and that salvation depends, not on rite, but on strenuous action upon oneself, on personal and persistent effort to reform oneself according to the Law. Such a principle of culture could not fully develop in Germany. It was in conflict with a certain atavic servility, and the tendency of the State to annex the absolute authority of God deflected its action. But in Anglo-Saxon countries it has had its full effect, and the idea of self-conquest and self-restraint remained alive. There it was that enterprises of moral reform by voluntary association and mutual incitement first made their appearance and achieved the greatest success; there, too, that responsible leaders can count, in a case of public need, on an appeal to conscience, conscience whose commands are not to be confused with those of honour. This power of the moral idea, this habit of spiritual discipline, are great advantages to a democracy. A people can govern itself better when many of its men are trained to self-government. And is not the energy and success of a people ever at one with the strength of its idea of duty ? In the last resort, is not its moral principle the whole of its vital principle ?

But in England, too, the beliefs that induced the habit of governing oneself according to the Law seem to be on the wane. In all the religious developments of the Reformation an element of rationalism is slowly at work, which ends by undermining the essential dogma —that very dogma which exhorted man to discipline as the means of salvation. Hence the recent progress of Catholicism in Protestant countries. Many souls in whom religious needs are strong, foreseeing where reasoning may lead, turn to the immutable Church which forbids free examination. There is already a great change among our neighbours, and Mr. Galsworthy recently ventured to write that hardly one Englishman in ten nowadays believes in a future life. A very different proportion to that we used to observe some thirty years ago, when there were almost as many men in church as women. More and more, in England as elsewhere, people are inclined to look for their Paradise here on earth ; hence the success of those doctrines which promise the masses that they will have it in this world. More and more the mystic faculty, roused by the undying need of faith in a better life, and ever alive in Anglo-Saxon countries, is turning to this promise. True, the impress of the old religion, a governing force among the dissenting people of the industrial regions, is still marked enough to astonish Continental Socialists, but such is the general trend, and we may well ask what the moral consequences will be. The pursuit of happiness, even of collective happiness, on this earth makes less for the training of conscience than the pursuit of salvation by self-discipline and reform. It may be objected that an acquired characteristic will remain acquired. But can we consider as really fixed a trait of historic origin, which we may call recent when we think of the myriads of years mankind has endured ? And can such a trait indefinitely survive the influence that produced it ? The strange and powerful character the English soul assumed at the time of the first Puritan preachings (there is no sign of it in Shakespeare)—a character that weakened in the eighteenth century, but revived at the beginning of the nineteenth—does not seem destined to last for ever.

In latter-day England no one has worked so faithfully for it as Kipling. This child of Bombay, who has felt the power of the East so deeply, is nevertheless the last of the English poets to champion the English idea of the self-governing soul directed by duty. I have quoted the verses entitled *Justice* at the end of his war poems—calling to account those who had broken the Law. In the same book there is yet another, of still more solemn inspiration, probably the last written, though it figures as the Dedication. This is *The Seven Watchmen*, the meaning of which we have already seen, but we must repeat the essential line here. To the Man in whom the Tempter tries to rouse the passion for power, the spirit of the Man whispers : " The Kingdom, the Kingdom is within you ! "

Thus, Kipling's first word is his last. After Armageddon, of which he had so long been thinking, as he looked back on all he had learnt and said of the good and evil of the war—pride, greed, bestiality, courage, patience, self-sacrifice — his final message is what he had taught in certain earnest, burning poems of his youth, that solemn conviction expressed in M'Andrew's hymn : Conscience, the ruler of the will, is the Absolute. The same idea, embodied in a crowd of living forms, had inspired all his work in the interval. A practical idea, therefore an unpoetical one, we shall be told by those who assume that art has no object beyond itself, that its true end is to enchant, not to serve life by purifying it and adding to its energy. But we must realise that this is the poetry of a world unlike our own, a world born of a different culture, and that, unless we shift our point of view for a moment, many of its moods will remain unintelligible to us. Greece had a poetry sometimes akin to dance, sometimes to contemplation. Palestine had another, aglow with the idea of the Eternal and His Law. And the profound difference between us and the English is that for generations they have been fed from childhood on the poetry of the Bible. " We are still the people of a single Book," said one of them to me ten years ago. It was almost an Islamic saying. Kipling's poetry emanates directly from the Book. If we sought to define it by contrast, we might oppose it to that of Baudelaire, so strange and disquieting in its dark poisonous splendour, so charged with insidious philtres, enervating and voluptuous fumes, dreams of death that paralyse action. The work of the English master is all alive, like an arrow loosed by a strong hand, and quivering with the faith and energy that propelled it. This burning desire for spiritual action Ruskin expressed in words that may shock artists and poets of another culture—but they forgive them if they know what perfection of art, what beauty of rhythm, he achieved in his prose, the finest prose in the English language. " A man," he said in his usual peremptory fashion, " has no business to write except to preach." In the main this idea still persists, even among those writers of his country who say nay to Puritan culture. A Galsworthy—and even a Wells—is still preaching when he shows up its harshness and intolerance, its unyielding prejudices. Great as is the former's art, he uses it for teaching, and I doubt if he would write had he no convictions to spread, no causes to defend. It matters little that these are diametrically opposed to those of Kipling.

But let us not make the mistake of reducing Kipling's poetry to a single strain, dominant though this may be. It is not always practical and austere in its inspiration. We have seen how he can vary it with fancy, humour and play—how he has played with children! We might point to a hundred pieces, the charm of which lies in the emotion and the beauty of the images and the rhythm, in the value of words chosen for their strong or tender music, their vivid imagery, or subtle suggestion. We might find others in which this poet —much more of a scholar than is commonly supposed —revived the grand Roman manner, the ceremonial and conceits of the Renaissance, the rhetorical gestures of our Revolution, the nervous brevity of American verse, the large, virile solemnities of the East.

These are but his amusements and his modes of speech. His essential quality is energy—an energy of which one might venture to say that it partakes of the driving power of the world—a will to live that devotes him to the service of life, and this, in his appointed order and place, in that England he serves as the leaf serves the tree from which it has received its form and law, and of which it bears in itself the essential sap. Better than any in our days he has represented the ancient culture, faith and ideal of this England. More than any he has feared and looked ahead for her, and when the hour of trial came he embodied her anguish and her will. Posterity, looking back and beholding the poet against the tragic background of our period, will see that his was the soul of his people.

But in fulfilling his mission he serves still higher and more general aims. If we wish to know his deeper purpose we should read some lines at the end of one of his early books, which indefinitely enlarge its scope and meaning :

> My new-cut ashlar takes the light
>   Where crimson-blank the windows flare ;
> By my own work, before the night,
>   Great Overseer, I make my prayer.

ENGLISH LITERATURE

If there be good in that I wrought
  Thy hand compelled it, Master, Thine ;
Where I have failed to meet Thy thought
  I know, through Thee, the blame is mine.

The depth and dream of my desire,
  The bitter paths wherein I stray,
Thou knowest, Who hast made the fire,
  Thou knowest, Who hast made the clay.

One stone the more swings to her place
  In that dread Temple of Thy worth.
It is enough that through Thy grace
  I saw naught common on Thy earth.

This stone, accurately cut for the Temple, is Kipling's
life-work—and by this prayer it is dedicated.

JOHN GALSWORTHY [1]

EVERY one has noted with interest the effort England began to make after the South African War to renew and adapt herself to modern conditions. Such activities are not confined to the practical and political domain ; they have their counterpart in a profound and general intellectual movement. It is not only the national forms of society that are called in question, but also the national forms of the mind : those prejudices, beliefs and traditions in which the fundamental ideas

[1] This study appeared in the *Revue des deux Mondes* in 1912. It deals with the five great novels Mr. Galsworthy had already published, a distinct and complete series in the work of the English master. They constitute a criticism of, or rather a very subtle satire on, English society, its types, morals, disciplines, ideas and prejudices as revealed in each of its leading categories. The first, *The Island Pharisees* (1904), presents a general view of the subject ; the second, *The Man of Property* (1906), the moneyed professional classes ; the third, *The Country House* (1907), the landed gentry ; the fourth, *Fraternity* (1909), the super-cultured, the intellectuals and writers ; the fifth, *The Patrician* (1911), the governing aristocracy.

The versatility of Mr. Galsworthy would be disconcerting to a critic intent on formulas. By his quick sense of what the subject and atmosphere of each novel or series of novels require, he attunes his art instinctively to their diversity. In the five important works we are about to study, where his attitude is that of the impassive observer and ironist, he is particularly subtle and secretive and very original in that correspond to ancient conditions of stability and life had perpetuated themselves. These very ideas were discussed, the essential principles of English culture, the scale of values they represent, and the types of humanity, so markedly distinct from other varieties of civilised man, which they have produced. To take a significant instance : certain writers now well known in France, a Bernard Shaw, a Chesterton, a Wells, have attacked the aristocratic and Christian conception of the *gentleman*, who reigned throughout the Victorian period, was glorified by moralists, typified by novelists in their heroes, and sung by the poets.

Among these thinkers there is one, the first as an artist, in my opinion, whose work is more difficult for foreigners to follow, because in the life of his characters he considers the most essential and sometimes the most

his reticences, at least to French readers. The appreciations attempted in the following pages refer more especially to this series.

Since *The Patrician*, Mr. Galsworthy has published several other novels (*The Dark Flower*, *The Freelands*, *Beyond*, *The Saint's Progress*), some pleading a cause, others dealing with phases of passion. Of these the infinitely delicate art is direct and explicit, developing in complete harmonies and in forms of perfect but more obvious beauty. There is a certain duality of inspiration in this writer, at once the most clear-sighted, the keenest of observers, and a being capable of deep emotion, readily moved to pity and indignation, and passionately devoted to certain causes.

Mr. Galsworthy has continued *The Man of Property*, first in the form of a short story (*The Indian Summer of a Forsyte* in *Five Tales*, 1918), and then in two novels (*In Chancery*, 1920, and *To Let*, 1921). This series forms what he has called *The Forsyte Saga*.

recondite moods of the English soul. This he does without making special studies of these moods, without defining and judging them, after the manner of Mr. Wells. He merely suggests them with tacit irony, fastening upon those fugitive expressions of character, the significance of which might well escape those who have no previous knowledge of this very special humanity. These types, whom he leaves us to identify, Mr. Galsworthy chooses in the most English portion of England, in that powerful governing class, the men of which, more accessible than the struggling majority to the determining influences of national culture, embody its ideas and keep them alive by their mutual suggestions. Of this class, which has so long been the active principle of the nation, determining its distinctive aspect and character ; of this essential England, of its various categories and types, noblemen, politicians, squires, priests of the Anglican Church, intellectuals, University men, rich merchants ; of the ideas of duty, customs, and class prejudices which fashion their souls and their persons, Mr. Galsworthy's novels are a most penetrating and methodical study, the more incisive because in secret he consistently opposes to the artificial, conventional and insular in the principles of English life the great elemental necessities which make man everywhere the same thing of Nature : Hunger, Love, Death.

I

He is a philosopher and a poet, a mystic poet, yet the most precise and systematic of realists. I write this last word without any idea of labelling him as belonging to a school ; I am not thinking of his manner, but of the object of his art, determined by his own point of view. It is that of all great artists possessed by the desire to seize and express complete reality, not only that which ordinary eyes perceive, but the deeper spiritual reality, the mystery of which haunts them, the power or the idea they divine beneath the appearance of a being or a thing, and try to reveal to us by their interpretation of that appearance. When the object of their study is man, they are chiefly concerned with his soul, in the vital depths and innermost life of which the external features are but symbols, that secret principle of harmony from which the form and movement of the creature proceed.

It is because he is so much interested in this human creature, because he is eager to see and show its secret workings, that he dwells upon all which explains and translates it to him. He is never weary of watching its aspects and gestures. In his art, what strikes one most at first is the fulness and accuracy of the concrete detail, a trait common to all the creations of the northern genius : a serious genius, worshipping spiritual beauty rather than plastic perfection, but reverencing truth too much to forget, in its yearning for the ideal, the complex irregularity of the real, or to force upon it the simplicity of abstract forms. If the hand that draws them were not so light and dexterous, Mr. Galsworthy's characters would make us think of the portraits painted by the early German masters. In both cases there is the same careful observation, the same sensibility to the infinitude of each human creature, and to that which is unique in each—some strange combination of traits in a soul and in a face which Nature will never repeat—the same attention to what is common to many men, expressive of type, age, class, and profession.

Hence the general tone of his work. Although inspired by a faith and instinct with love and pity, it has all the calm, all the precise and deliberate serenity, of pure observation. No great English novelist of our times has shown so little of himself in his books. We find in them nothing akin to Dickens' outbursts of high spirits or emotion, to George Eliot's discursive sermonising, to Meredith's fantasies, or the lyric ardour, the sudden tension of energy, the lightning flashes, of Kipling. Nothing but a series of quiet little touches by an unerring brush, each amazingly expressive, complementary to all the others, helping to suggest the relation of a certain face, certain bodily habits, a certain physiology, to certain rhythms of will, thought and feeling. When this degree of realisation is reached, intuitive imagination can dispense with the plot of the novel. The creator of the Forsytes can use the painter's privilege and restrict himself to the study of a figure. As long as it is significant and individual, put together in accordance with the inner logic of life, as long as vitality is suggested alike in the colour of the eyes, the lustre or eclipse of the look, the pallor or flush of the complexion, the energy, languor or serenity of the expression, the indolence or the decision of the attitude, the artist is certain to interest us, especially when beneath these individual characteristics a specific element is revealed, the mark of a particular culture, the *parti pris* of a particular civilisation. Mr. Galsworthy has written books which are not mere collections of elaborate portraits, but which tell us all there is to know about contemporary English types.

One of these books[1] begins with a study of some twenty pages called *A Portrait*, where we see, organically realised in a vivid figure, a certain idea of life that has counted for a good deal in the substance of modern England. This stately old man, whose back is not yet bent, who holds his head so high, whose deep eyes, so straight and steady in their gaze, have kept their sparkle and their iron-gray colour ; this octogenarian, with beautiful silver hair, broad calm forehead, jaw of great determination and prominent chin cleft by a dimple, is an English gentleman of the upper middle classes who has lived nearly the whole of the nineteenth century. His fundamental quality, balance : balance of the powers of sentiment and thought, and the energies of will and action. He is rich ; he respects wealth, to him the token and the fruit of a laborious and well-regulated life. He has worked hard, never too hard. Morally, he is self-sufficing. He has not a very original mind, but he does not rely upon the opinion of others ; he has his convictions, his philosophy, his ethics, which translate his natural tendencies as an Englishman and gentleman, and his experience of life. He despises everything that savours of languor and weakness, or of insolent and brutal force. His past, his tastes and

[1] *A Motley.*

habits, are described, his sunny, spacious country house, so carefully planned with a view to the health and pleasure of his children, his artistic tastes, of the classic order.   In literature, his favourites are George Eliot and Turgenev, and he dislikes Meredith and Browning ;   in music, he has tried to understand Wagner, but nothing delights him like the happy, radiant perfection of Mozart ; in painting, he has not followed Ruskin and the Pre-Raphaelites ; he has not gone so far as Botticelli, and he distrusts Turner. Then we hear of his deep English feeling for Nature. How strongly he is moved by a pretty face, a beautiful figure, a mellow tune, the moon behind a poplar tree, a blackbird's song. or a starry night, when he stands silent or perhaps says wistfully, looking heavenwards : " What little bits of things we are !   Poor little wretches ! "   These moods he once tried to express in the naïve stilted poetic efforts of his early days, the secret of which he has never revealed.   Thus, gradually the figure is built up before us by means of the innumerable little traits selected, all showing something of the same fundamental quality.   We are told how he dresses, of his somewhat rococo style of cricket, which he is fond of playing with his grandchildren, the kind of tea he prefers, his attitude to the poor.   We see him in his office, in the children's nursery, where he is happiest ; in church, which he attends regularly from a sense of decorum and social discipline ; in the churchyard, where with bowed head he meditates, by the graveside of a friend, on the death which is drawing very near for himself ; and when we come to the last page, we know him through and through. He impresses us as the rare and perfect specimen of a species, the typical son of an age which was that of Thackeray and Tennyson, one which the more critical children of a new period may deride for its lack of logic and its intellectual timidity, but may well regret, too, when they feel their own weakness and unrest, and realise the effort it will cost them to adapt themselves morally and socially to the conditions of the coming world. His was a century between two ages, when England, ingenuous and illogical, still clung to forms evolved during periods of faith and authority, never suspecting that these forms were doomed. Her men were still healthy and at peace " in the shade of the ancient oak which had been cut through at the roots."

In the great novels the figures are shown in movement, but the detail is as minute as ever. The drama, often relegated to the middle distance, is meant only to bring them out completely, to present them in all their moods, with all the possible gestures of living men, with the hidden current of thought and sentiment, the rhythm of which is as proper to each as his way of walking or the sound of his voice. The pathetic happenings, love, death, nature, are there but to suggest ironically, by the contrast of the eternal powers, all that is limited, individual and local in the type described and the ideas which govern it. The essential element in *The Man of Property* is the natural history of the Forsytes, a family the various generations of which represent the virtues and defects typical of the great upper middle class of England in the nineteenth century

—energy, invincible vitality, worship of health, taciturn pride, secret determination not to give oneself away, irreducible egotism, passion for property, tendency to appreciate everything in terms of money, open contempt for ideas, jealous individualism strangely combined with a superstitious respect for conventions and hostility to all who deviate from the prescribed and recognised pattern. The real subject of the book is James Forsyte, Jolyon Forsyte, Swithin Forsyte, Roger, Nicholas and Timothy Forsyte, their sisters, their wives, their children, their nephews, each a variety of the general type of Forsytes, that is to say, the professional gentry of England.

Such a book may almost be classified as zoology. It is a series of pictures in which a certain family presents both its specific and its individual features. Its various characters are seen in the principal situations of human life, and the special situations in the life of an Englishman of the upper middle classes. The very titles of the chapters : " *At Home* " *at old Jolyon's, Dinner at Swithin's, Drive with Swithin, Old Jolyon at the Opera, Death of Aunt Anne, Dance at Roger's, Evening at Richmond Park,* sufficiently indicate the author's point of view—that of methodical observation. When you read the novel, you see Soames suspecting and watching his wife, making up his mind with secret greed and calculation to an operation of supreme importance in the Forsyte world—the purchasing of an estate ; you see him defending his purse, bringing an action against the hated rival who has thrust himself into his home, answering with astonishing self-control, in curt, contemptuous phrases, the insidious questions put to him by his adversary's counsel. You see Swithin, the rough-hewn massive bachelor of seventy-five, threatened by apoplexy, but proud of his horses, his wines and cigars, pondering deeply over the menu of a dinner. You are present at the Board meeting presided over by the octogenarian Jolyon; you accompany him to the theatre, to the sea-side, to his club and town house; you surprise the secret of his wistful loneliness. You note the various aspects of his person, what he is with his brothers, his son, and his grandchildren— arrogant, distrustful, scornful in some of these relations; simple, sensitive and even furtively weak in others. You understand the obscure terror all these Forsytes feel at the thought of such a monstrous scandal as an adultery in the family, and learn that in England an injured husband is not a comic figure. You follow them to the funeral of Aunt Anne, who has died only that you may note, beneath the mechanical gestures of convention, the intimate reactions of these stubborn, grasping Englishmen confronted with the corpse of one of their own kin. Here you see their idea of death, as you have already seen their conceptions of happiness, honour, morality religion, marriage, family ties, love, art, and now you may appreciate all the characteristics of their species, a numerous one in England; you understand how by one of those odd mixtures of contraries produced by life, that species is a combination of the aristocratic and the vulgar, the commercial and the puritanical, the gregarious and the individualistic, the haughty and the mean, the primitive and the over-civilised.

JOHN GALSWORTHY

Thus Mr. Galsworthy handles his characters, varying the silhouette each time he presents it, that we may learn to know them in the delicate, shifting complexity proper even to the simplest creature, and this by a series of experiences, similar to those which in real life build up and correct our knowledge of our fellows. He is careful not to describe them exhaustively— showing at first only the most salient features, and giving us but a summary impression. He allows them to reveal themselves in infinite gradation by their speech and bearing, by their perception of one another, expressed by each in his own words and images—above all, by that series of sensations, ideas, dreams, whims, decisions which the author never seems to be following and noting from without, never transposes into mono- logue, but presents by means of a device to which English is admirably suited—indirect speech. By this device, which does not claim to register a regular suc- cession of mental words—an unusual phenomenon— but attempts to reproduce the movements of a soul, Mr. Galsworthy's creatures become transparent to us. We can watch the working of their internal mechanism.

It is difficult to give any idea of such an art by fragments, for the writer makes his characters so real and living to us that we should recognise them if we came across them ; and this he does by the cumulative effect of many touches, each of which gets its full value only with the context. Nevertheless, we must quote, for in criticism this is the only way in which we can give a definite impression.

Here, for instance, we have old Jolyon, a business

man, the eldest of the family, over eighty, superbly hale and hearty. With his dome-like forehead, his shrewd, steady eyes, his immense white moustache drooping below his strong jaw, he seems, in spite of hollow cheeks and temples, the master of perennial youth—a youth not uncommon among the old men of the strong English upper middle class. Jolyon is the finest of the Forsytes, the only one with something large and generous in his nature, proud, domineering and contemptuous, but so far differing from the family type that he is capable of tenderness and disinterested vision, though the tradition of his caste compels him to conceal his sensibilities. He is very lonely. Yielding one evening to a long-stifled yearning of his heart, he has paid a visit to his son, young Jolyon, whom he has not seen for years, because the latter had broken the strictest canon of a society, still essentially puritan, by an irregular connection which had estranged him from his kin. The house and the neighbourhood seem to him second-rate, unworthy of the son who bears his name. To this old Englishman everything marked with the stamp of poverty spells shame, and young Jolyon is poor; he has proudly refused money help from a father who had disowned him. The interview in the little garden was embarrassing; the woman, silent and agitated, looked at him with an air of fear and resentment. All of a sudden, shaken with sobs, she got up and hurried into the house, followed by her husband. Old Jolyon was left alone with the children, whom he had never seen before; they climbed up on his knees, and their innocent grace attracted him

strangely; the stubborn old man had always had a
tenderness for little children. When his son came back,
he restrained himself; his English shyness and habitual
reserve made it impossible for him to speak out.
Nothing was said as to a future visit. Now he goes
back to his own home, sad and dissatisfied.

" What a poor, miserable place! And he thought of
the great empty house at Stanhope Gate, fit residence
for a Forsyte, with its huge billiard-room and drawing-
room that no one entered from one week's end to
another.

That woman, whose face he had rather liked, was
too thin-skinned by half! She gave Jo a bad time, he
knew. And those sweet children! Ah! what a piece
of awful folly!

He walked towards the Edgware Road between
rows of little houses, all suggesting to him (erroneously,
no doubt, but the prejudices of a Forsyte are sacred)
shady histories of some kind or another.

Society, forsooth, the chattering hags and jackanapes,
had set themselves up to pass judgment on *his* flesh
and blood. A parcel of old women! He stumped his
umbrella on the ground as though to drive it into the
heart of that unfortunate body which had dared to
ostracise his son and his son's son, in whom he could
have lived again!

He stumped his umbrella fiercely; yet he himself
had followed Society's behaviour for fifteen years—
had only to-day been false to it.

He thought of June and her dead mother, and the
whole story with all his old bitterness. A wretched
business!

He was a long time reaching Stanhope Gate, for with
native perversity, being extremely tired, he walked the
whole way.

After washing his hands in the lavatory downstairs he went to the dining-room to wait for dinner, the only room he used when June was out—it was less lonely so. The evening paper had not yet come ; he had finished the *Times*, there was therefore nothing to do.

The room faced the backwater of traffic, and was very silent. He disliked dogs, but a dog even would have been company. His gaze, travelling round the walls, rested on a picture entitled : *Group of Dutch Fishing Boats at Sunset*, the *chef d'œuvre* of his collection. It gave him no pleasure. He closed his eyes. He was lonely. He oughtn't to complain, he knew, but he couldn't help it. He was a poor thing—had always been a poor thing—no pluck ! Such was his thought.

The butler came to lay the table for dinner, and seeing his master apparently asleep, exercised extreme caution in his movements. This bearded man also wore a moustache which had given rise to grave doubts in the minds of many members of the family, especially those who like Soames had been to public schools, and were accustomed to niceness in such matters. Could he really be considered a butler ? Playful spirits alluded to him as Uncle Jolyon's Nonconformist.

He moved to and fro between the great polished sideboard and the great polished table, inimitably sleek and soft.

Old Jolyon watched him, feigning sleep. The fellow was a sneak—he had always thought so—who cared about nothing but rattling through his work and getting out to his betting or his woman, or goodness knew what ! A slug ! Fat, too ! And didn't care a pin about his master.

But then against his will came one of those moments of philosophy which made old Jolyon different from other Forsytes.

After all, why should the man care ? He wasn't

paid to care, and why expect it ? In this world people couldn't look for affection unless they paid for it. It might be different in the next—he didn't know, he couldn't tell ! And again he shut his eyes.

Relentless and stealthy, the butler pursued his labours, taking things from the various compartments by the sideboard. His back seemed always turned to old Jolyon ; thus, he robbed his operations of the unseemliness of being carried on in his master's presence ; now and then he furtively breathed on the silver and wiped it with a piece of chamois leather. He appeared to pore over the quantities of wine in the decanters which he carried carefully and rather high, letting his beard droop over them protectingly. When he had finished he stood for over a minute watching his master, and in his greenish eyes there was a look of contempt.

After all, this master of his was an old buffer, who hadn't much left in him !

Soft as a tom-cat, he crossed the room to press the bell. His orders were ' dinner at seven.' What if his master were asleep ; he would soon have him out of that ; there was the night to sleep in ! He had himself to think of, for he was due at his Club at half-past eight.

In answer to the ring appeared a page boy with a silver soup tureen. The butler took it from his hands and placed it on the table ; then, standing by the open door as though about to usher company into the room, he said in a solemn voice :

' Dinner is on the table, sir.'

Slowly old Jolyon got up out of his chair, and sat down at the table to eat his dinner."

What strikes us in this scene is not only the wealth of psychological detail, but the minute description of the setting—necessary when types are to be presented. For a type is not to be characterised merely by physical and moral structure. A man exists only in relation to his surroundings, which he has fashioned, and which help to fashion him, or, at least, to keep him true to himself. In *The Country House* and *The Man of Property* trivial externals are described with a minuteness which a reader inattentive to the psychological under-current of the novel might think tedious. If Mr. Galsworthy tells us of a dinner-party—that, for instance, where Soames, Irene, June and Bosinney are brought together —he indicates the places occupied by each ; he gives us the menu : the soup, " excellent, if a little thick " ; the fish, " a fine fresh sole from Dover " ; cutlets, " pink-frilled about the legs," an apple charlotte ; he suggests the quality of the olives, the wines, the coffee, the cigarettes. If Soames remarks, " *You'll find the champagne dry, the charlotte is good* " ; if the servant murmurs, " *Salad, sir ?* " ; if June asks for sugar, he does not fail to note it. He even records the silences. I almost hesitate to quote such a scene lest the reader should shrug his shoulders and speak of photographic art.

II

Yet I shall quote it, for here we see the novelist's second and most interesting method. Mr. Galsworthy makes use of two opposite devices simultaneously ; one consists in saying everything, the other in not saying everything. And this he is able to do, for often —here we have the most original feature of his art— the reality with which he is dealing for the moment is dual, and works out on two different planes. The while he carefully follows a certain order of facts, he leaves us to guess at another from certain minute but carefully selected indications. Generally, the latter is the more moving, being the passion or the action of the main characters, which he likes to suggest by fragments that call adroitly upon our imagination to fill in the gaps.

Such a method is the outcome of a conception of art directly opposed to one long dominant in France. Writers of our romantic and pseudo-realistic schools have never quite forgotten their rhetoric, the incomparable models which Racine's tragedies offer us in their alternating speeches. If natural speech is made to express thought, the French generally hold that written speech should express it more completely and in a more perfect order ; hence the ideal of good writing by which our public judges even the dialogue in a play or a novel. The English, more indifferent to logic, have tried above all to express the real, complex and fragmentary, and in their conception of the real they include the many-sided world of the mind—a reality ignored by the realistic Zola. Hence an idea of the dialogue peculiar to their psychological novelists. In a conversation, many of the movements of the soul are hidden, many silences are expressive, many words in themselves insignificant take on a strong and novel meaning, vital with the life of the interlocutors, and convey to them something not to be found in the dictionary. If we really know the secret psychology of the characters (and Mr. Galsworthy is so interested in it that rather than explain and describe he likes to show us the events, landscapes, and even

the figures of his story in the images of these reflected
in the particular mind he is dealing with), if we have
grasped the situation, the slightest words are enough
to suggest, as in real life, the unexpressed thoughts they
conceal.

The advantages of the method are obvious. It has
a peculiar power; the thing of which we catch half-
mysterious glimpses gains in effect, and is charged with
emotion which would evaporate in the crude light of
the foreground. The illusion of reality is produced,
the foreground being occupied by ordinary people and
things, while trifles mask matters of profound import.
Finally, it appeals to our intelligence, urging us to
think. It is not the author, but we ourselves who
observe and interpret. What a pleasure it is to watch
the characters, to guess all that is concealed! What
amusing discoveries we make!

Let us now turn our attention to our dinner party.
Soames, the host, is a perfect specimen of the social
category studied in *The Man of Property*. Forty years
old: tall, well shaven, with flat cheeks, cold, watchful
gray eyes, a general air of pallor and precision. An old
Etonian, which neither his father nor his uncles had
been; imbued like them with a haughty respect for
those appearances which denote success among men of
his caste, but better posted in the latest subtleties of
fashion and etiquette. A suspicious, crafty fellow,
hiding his money transactions, measuring everything
in pounds, shillings and pence, a man of property in
his soul, and looking upon his wife as one of his possessions. Irene, his wife, a strange, beautiful creature,

with dark eyes in curious contrast to her golden hair—
a sign, it appears, of weak will ; silent, instinctive,
passive, of another species in the midst of the energetic
and practical Forsytes, where she is stifled ; a mysterious flower, a closed flower hitherto, now opening
unconsciously in the presence of Bosinney, and sending
out a disturbing, intoxicating perfume towards him.
Bosinney, the architect, June's lover, drifting away
rapidly from her under this bewildering influence, a
dreamer regardless of all the conventions, standards
and codes of the English gentry, now absorbed in his
dream, now suddenly alive to their calculations, full
of irony towards these vain, possessive, rigid Philistines ;
a penniless Bohemian with an oblique profile, prominent
brows and cheek-bones, hollow cheeks and curly dark
hair ; a man who had paid his duty calls on the family
after the engagement in a soft gray hat (a hat the
Forsytes instinctively felt to be " dangerous, ah,
dangerous ! ") ; the man of whom Jolyon's coachman had
said : " Dunno what to make of 'im. Looks to me for
all the world like an 'alf tame leopard " ; the man the
huge Swithin calls " a bumpy beggar " ; whom the dreary
James, disconcerted by his secret, sarcastic smile, his
mysterious air, his soft, feline footfall, had described
as looking like " a hungry cat." Beside him, June,
who loves him, the slender, vehement, self-willed grand
daughter of Jolyon, whose chin and courage she has
inherited, a little creature " all hair and spirit," with a
neck that seems too slight to carry her heavy crown of
bright hair. Note the keenness of perception shown
by these details scattered here and there in the course

of the narrative and the dialogues. Mr. Galsworthy, a profound student of the life of the soul, is alive to its physical substructure. So was Shakespeare, when in *Hamlet* the Queen remarks of her son : " He's fat and scant of breath."

And now for the situation. For some time past, June has been feeling dimly that her lover is slipping away from her, and she has counted upon this evening to draw him back. On arriving at Soames' house, she has overheard a few whispered words exchanged between her cousin Irene and Bosinney as she entered the drawing-room—innocent words, for neither of the pair has as yet recognised the nature of the force that is drawing them together—but words spoken in a concentrated tone of fervour and intimacy—a revelation to the girl's uneasiness, which will presently flame into jealousy.

We can now follow the conversation at the dinner table. Disjointed, trivial speeches, hardly worth noting, it would seem, reveal intimate depths of emotion, a whole world of dreams and passion.

" Dinner began in silence ; the women facing one another and the men.

In silence the soup was finished—excellent, if a little thick ; and fish was brought. In silence it was handed.

Bosinney ventured : ' It's the first spring day.'

Irene echoed softly : ' Yes—the first spring day.'

' Spring ! ' said June, ' there isn't a breath of air.' No one replied.

The fish was taken away, a fine fresh sole from Dover. And Bilson brought champagne, a bottle swathed around the neck with white.

Soames said : ' You'll find it dry.'

Cutlets were handed, each pink frilled about the legs. They were refused by June and silence fell. ·

Soames said : ' You'd better take a cutlet, June ; there's nothing coming.'

But June again refused, so they were borne away. And then Irene asked : ' Phil, have you heard my blackbird ? '

Bosinney answered : ' Rather—he's got a hunting song. As I came round I heard him in the square.'

' He's such a darling ! '

' Salad, sir ? ' Spring chicken was removed.

But Soames was speaking : ' The asparagus is very poor. Bosinney, glass of sherry with your sweet. June, you're drinking nothing ! '

June said : ' You know I never do. Wine's such horrid stuff.'

An apple-charlotte came upon a silver dish. And smilingly Irene said : ' The azaleas are so wonderful this year.'

To this Bosinney murmured : ' Wonderful ! The scent's extraordinary.'

June said : ' How *can* you like the scent ? Sugar, please, Bilson.'

Sugar was handed her and Soames remarked : ' The charlotte's good.'

The charlotte was removed. Long silence followed. Irene, beckoning, said : ' Take out the azalea, Bilson. Miss June can't bear the scent.'

' No, let it stay,' said June.

Olives from France with Russian caviare were placed on little plates. And Soames remarked : ' Why can't we have the Spanish ? ' But no one answered.

The olives were removed. Lifting her tumbler June demanded : ' Give me some water, please.' Water was given her. A silver tray was brought, with German plums. There was a lengthy pause. In perfect harmony all were eating them.

Bosinney counted up the stones. ' This year, next year, some time—— '

Irene finished softly : ' Never. There was such a glorious sunset. The sky's all ruby still—so beautiful.'

He answered : ' Underneath the dark.'

Their eyes had met and June cried scornfully : ' A London sunset ! '

Egyptian cigarettes were handed in a silver box. Soames, taking one, remarked : ' What time does your play begin ? '

No one replied, and Turkish coffee followed in enamelled cups.

Irene, smiling quietly, said : ' If only—— '

' Only what ? ' said June.

' If only it could always be the spring ! '

Brandy was handed ; it was pale and old.

Soames said : ' Bosinney, better take some brandy.'

Bosinney took a glass ; they all arose.

' You want a cab ? ' asked Soames.

June answered : ' No. My cloak, please, Bilson.' Her cloak was brought.

Irene from the window murmured : ' Such a lovely night. The stars are coming out ! '

Soames added : ' Well, I hope you'll both enjoy yourselves.'

From the door June answered : ' Thanks. Come, Phil.'

Bosinney cried : ' I'm coming.'

Soames smiled a sneering smile and said : ' I wish you luck.'

And at the door Irene watched them go.

Bosinney called : ' Good night.'

' Good night,' she answered softly.

June made her lover take her on the top of a 'bus, saying she wanted air, and there sat silent, with her face to the breeze."

I should think she did want air. Her head must have been afire.

Unless the whole trend of the novel has prepared us for this scene, it will not be easy for us to follow the secret currents of passion that cross one another here. Let us turn back to it and glance again at certain details. The beginning seems insignificant enough. Yet passion is already expressing itself imperceptibly.

"Bosinney ventured : ' It's the first spring day.'
Irene echoed softly : ' Yes—the first spring day.'
' Spring ! ' said June, ' there isn't a breath of air ! ' "

Three little sentences that probably cause the husband no uneasiness; but enough to betray the drama that is being enacted between the three inter- locutors, and to give us the key to their souls. Does not the reader feel the dreamy languor of the future lovers who are bewitching each other ? They are conscious of the spring, because they are in that strange mood when man is attuned to Nature (note further Irene's murmured words about the flowers, the sunset, the night and stars). " The first day of spring ! "—the first day of their love, too, of those mute avowals June has just surprised. Irene echoes the young man's words ; she is passive, magnetised ; she speaks low. Then suddenly, cutting through the current established between them, the abrupt contradiction of the exas- perated little *fiancée :* " Spring ! there isn't a breath of air."

The theme has thus been given and the trio proceed to work out the variations. When Irene breaks the

silence and says with her mysterious smile : " The
azaleas are so wonderful this year," no doubt the smile
is vague ; she thinks of the azaleas in the conservatory
—" wonderful " because it was among them that she
felt herself so near Bosinney. And when he replies :
" Yes, wonderful ! The scent's extraordinary ! " he,
too, speaks in a murmur, in a dream, and speaks but for
her. And again June's impatient exclamation inter-
rupts the current setting from Irene to the young man.
" How *can* you like the scent ? " For it was behind
the azaleas that she had broken in upon their con-
fidences. She loathes the scent now. And we may be
sure there is something strained and unnatural in her
voice when she adds in the same breath : " Sugar,
please, Bilson ! " A moment later her agitation
betrays itself again. " Take out the azalea, Bilson,
Miss June can't bear the scent." " No, let it stay,"
says June. Sheer nervous irritation ! She is suffo-
cating ; she cannot eat : she refuses the dishes offered
her.

Now read to the end of the scene, the pathos of which
rises as it advances. What melancholy foreboding in
these words of Bosinney's and Irene's : " This year—
next year—some time—never ! The sky's all ruby still
—so beautiful ! "—" Yes, underneath the dark." . . .
And then : " If only . . . " said Irene softly.—" Only
what ? " breaks in June ; meaning, Speak up !—speak
to us all.—" If only it could always be the spring ! "—
That is to say, if this moment could last for ever, if there
were no black, threatening future ! Finally, note how
in this scene of passion the psychology of each character

is sustained. Irene is the same passive, sensitive, reticent creature we have seen hitherto. June is the self-willed little granddaughter of old Jolyon ; her reactions are those of courage and attack. Bosinney, the lover, is also the artist who had noticed that the blackbird whistled a hunting song. In Soames we behold the eternal husband, and further, the precise and positive Forsyte, intent on present and material realities, who keeps an eye on the clock and suggests a cab ; the sharp-eyed man who sees nothing, the man of property as host, commenting on his dinner—who knows the menu and the cellar. Every touch here is significant. When the guests leave, June has to call Bosinney : " Come, Phil." He cries : " I'm coming." He " cries," no doubt, because when Soames and June went to the door he lingered in the drawing-room with Irene. We can imagine what this evening's pleasure-making of an engaged couple will be like. You have seized the subtle intention in the following passage : " *A silver tray was brought, with German plums. There was a lengthy pause. In perfect harmony all were eating them.*" For a moment the author stands away from his characters and looks at them from outside. What he sees and shows us, ironically, is the satisfactory spectacle of a united family at dinner. The " lengthy pause " was worth noting. There seem to have been many pauses ; something ominous is hanging over this dinner.

Now in place of this written commentary—writing is always so slow and heavy !—imagine the quick flashes of insight, the brief, searching visions of under-

lying psychology that illumine each word of this scene
for the reader who has been led to it by all the preceding
chapters, and you will begin to realise the subtlety and
achievements of this art. What breaks through the
surface here together with the inner life of the characters
is the secret life of the whole novel at a certain stage of
its development. For beneath the study of the
Forsytes, through the series of typical scenes which
reveal them in the main aspects of their breed, the
novel moves on, advancing slowly and surely, by a fatal
and necessary progress towards its climax of passion.
This progress is almost invisible, " subterranean," as
the members of the family themselves say breathlessly,
referring to the alarming and mysterious affair of Irene
and Bosinney. Of the twelve or fifteen people who
figure in *The Man of Property*, the two lovers are those
of whom we see least. They stand aside in the wings,
whence their movements are revealed only by their
shadows thrown on the back-cloth. If they appear
upon the stage incidentally, some trivial circumstance
brings them forward together with other characters ;
we never see them *tête-à-tête* save for that brief moment
when June is watching them ; their passion is not
expressed before us. It is the wonder of this art that
while the tragedy is kept almost out of our sight, its
emotion is so passed on to us that a strange and deadly
perfume seems to be rising throughout the novel from
this hidden flower of love, penetrating all the cold,
positive and correct English life that overlies it. And
by an effect of the same miracle, these two remote
figures, wrapt in shade behind so many others we see

speaking and acting in the foreground, are just the
only ones who haunt us like the memory of a vision.
We cannot forget their pale earnestness, their strange-
ness, their predestined air, as if they were possessed
and dedicate, their attitude of passive submission to the
power older than mankind which is leading them on to
their fate—and finally, their solitude in the midst of a
society where they have ceased to represent anything,
because henceforth they belong only to eternal Nature.

III

When we read the novel for the second time—the
first time we only feel its effect—we begin to understand
the miracle. The love-story is revealed to us *through
the characters* the author places in the foreground of
his stage—those types he has studied with such penetrating attention. It is through what each of these,
by virtue of his position and psychological structure,
sees of the drama that *we* see the drama and the two
protagonists. Hence a curious feature of Mr. Galsworthy's subtle and intricate art. At every moment
we find him simultaneously working out several
characters. At the same time that he shows a certain
aspect, a certain decisive gesture of one of the tragic
figures, he studies more deeply some subordinate,
average and sometimes comic character. The special
distortion the image of the first undergoes by refraction
through the second gives us a new view of the latter.
The wonder is that, passing through this medium, the
drama subsists and gradually develops its powers of

emotion. This is how the most momentous meeting between Irene and Bosinney is presented to us in *The Man of Property*.

One of Soames' uncles, the biggest, most massive and elemental of the Forsytes, whose outlook upon the world has remained simpler than that of the others, Swithin, a septuagenarian, bulky, over six feet in height, impatient and overbearing, but heavy and stiff with age, and with a tendency to apoplexy, has taken it into his head to ask Irene to drive with him. He imagines that she is fond of him, that she is the only one who understands him. At her request he has taken her to Robin Hill, where Bosinney, the architect, who is building a house for Soames, had entreated her to come and see him. The old beau has made a point of driving her himself, for he has a reputation as a horsey man. He is got up very smartly in honour of the pretty woman who is to be his companion, wears a pair of dogskin gloves, and exhales a fragrance of opoponax and cigars. He keeps looking at Irene out of the corner of his eye, for all the world like a solemn old peacock. The next day, in his brother Timothy's drawing-room, where the old aunts meet, he describes the drive. His narrative, broken by dumb rumination, the occasional shrillness of his voice, his lapses into silence, which he tries to make expressive by rolling his eyes; his impatience, his flashes of insight, confused and sudden as the rushes of blood that crimson his face—all these wonderfully suggest the physiology of this old Forsyte.

" Irene came out at once, and stepped into the phaeton 'as light as—er—Taglioni, no fuss about it, no

wanting this or wanting that,' and above all, Swithin
dwelt on this, staring at Mrs. Septimus in a way that
disconcerted her a good deal, 'no silly nervousness.'

To Aunt Hester he portrayed Irene's hat. ' Not one
of your great flopping things, sprawling about and
catching the dust, that women are so fond of nowadays,
but a neat little '—he made a circular motion of his
hand—' white veil—capital taste.'

' What was it made of ? ' inquired Aunt Hester,
who manifested a languid but permanent excitement at
any mention of dress.

' Made of ? ' returned Swithin ; ' now how should
I know ? '

He sank into a silence so profound that Aunt Hester
began to be afraid he had fallen into a trance. . . .

On the Sunday morning Swithin had opened his eyes
at the mention of Robin Hill ; it was a long way for
his horses, and he always dined at half-past seven,
before the rush at the Club began ; the new *chef* took
more trouble with an early dinner—a lazy rascal !
He would like to have a look at the house, however.
A house appealed to any Forsyte, and especially to one
who had been an auctioneer. After all, he said, the
distance was nothing. When he was a younger man
he had had rooms at Richmond for many years, kept
his carriage and pair there, and drove them up and down
to business every day of his life. ' Four-in-hand
Forsyte,' they called him. His T-cart, his horses had
been known from Hyde Park Corner to the ' Star and
Garter.' The Duke of Z—— wanted to get hold of
them, would have given him double the money, but
he had kept them ; know a good thing when you have
it, eh ? A look of solemn pride came portentously on
his shaven, square old face ; he rolled his head in his
stand-up collar, like a turkey-cock preening himself."

The splendid old turkey-cock spreads his tail, too,

for he is convinced that Irene is fascinated by him.
" Her dark eyes shone so in the spring light, and whenever he spoke she raised them to him and smiled." A
silent smile of dreamy happiness ; every minute was
bringing her nearer to Bosinney.

He was very tired when they got to Robin Hill.
A life-time of careful deportment had alone kept his
tall and bulky form from falling askew towards the end
of the drive. Guided by Bosinney he enters the new
house with the young woman. His valet has put his
gold-mounted Malacca cane into his hand, for his old
knees are feeling the effects of their long stay in the
same position. He has also put on his fur coat to
guard against draughts.

They go over the house—a house conceived by a
modern artist—which Swithin sees with the eyes of a
Forsyte, a Philistine who was in his prime in 1850, and
has retained the tastes of his day.

" The staircase, he said, was handsome ! the baronial
style ! They would want some statuary about ! He
came to a standstill between the columns of the door-
way into the inner court, and held out his cane
inquiringly.
What was this to be ?—this vestibule, or whatever
they called it. But gazing at the skylight, inspiration
came to him.
' Ah ! the billiard-room ! '
When told it was to be a tiled court with plants in
the centre, he turned to Irene :
' Waste this on plants ! You take my advice and
have a billiard table here ! '
Irene smiled. She had lifted her veil, banding it
like a nun's coif across her forehead, and the smile of

her dark eyes below this seemed to Swithin more charming than ever. He nodded. She would take his advice, he saw."

Finally, he asks for a chair, and settles on the terrace, telling Bosinney to take Irene and show her the house from below, while he sits and looks at the view.

" He sat down by the oak tree, in the sun ; square and upright, with one hand stretched out, resting on the knob of his cane . . . his fur coat thrown open, his hat roofing with its flat top the pale square of his face ; his stare, very blank, fixed on the landscape.
They went off down the fields. He was, indeed, not sorry to be left thus for a quiet moment of reflection. The air was balmy, not too much heat in the sun ; the prospect a fine one, a remarka——. His head fell a little to one side ; he jerked it up and thought : Odd ! They were waving to him from the bottom. He put up his hand and moved it more than once. They were active. The prospect was remarka——. His head fell to the left, he jerked it up at once ; it fell to the right. It remained there ; he was asleep."

He sleeps, while Irene and Bosinney disappear into the wood, full of flowers and young shoots. The air is sweet with the scent of hawthorn and mint ; a cuckoo is calling in the distance. They wander away, alone, far from the world, lovers in the bosom of free Nature, amidst the scents and languors of the Spring. What their walk may be the author leaves us to imagine.

" Swithin awoke ; virtue had gone out of him. He had a taste in his mouth. Where was he ?
Damme ! He had been asleep !

He had dreamt something about a new soup with a taste of mint in it.

These young people—where had they got to ? His left leg had pins and needles.

' Adolf ! ' The rascal was not there ; the rascal was asleep somewhere.

He stood up, tall, square, bulky in his fur, looking anxiously down over the fields, and presently he saw them coming.

Irene was in front ; the young fellow—what had they nicknamed him ?—' The Buccaneer ? '—looked precious hang-dog there behind her ; had got a flea in his ear he shouldn't wonder. Serve him right, taking her all that way down to look at the house. . . .

They had stopped. What were they standing there for, talking, talking ? They came on again. She had been giving him a rub, he had not the least doubt of it, and no wonder, over a house like that, a great, ugly thing. . . . He looked intently at their faces with his pale, immovable stare. The young man looked very queer !

' You'll never make anything of this ! ' he said tartly, pointing at the mansion ; ' too new-fangled.'

Bosinney gazed at him as though he had not heard ; and Swithin afterwards described him to Aunt Hester as ' an extravagant sort of fellow—very odd way of looking at you—a bumpy beggar ! '

What gave rise to this sudden piece of psychology he did not state ; possibly Bosinney's prominent forehead and cheek-bones and chin, or something hungry in his face, which quarrelled with Swithin's conception of the calm satiety that should characterise the perfect gentleman.

He brightened up at the mention of tea. He had a contempt for tea—his brother Jolyon had been in tea ; made a lot of money by it—but he was so thirsty, and had such a taste in his mouth that he was prepared to drink anything. He longed to inform Irene of the taste in his mouth—she was so sympathetic—but it would not be a distinguished thing to do ; he rolled his tongue round, and faintly smacked it against his palate.''

Instead of tea they give him champagne, and we shall see the sudden illumination produced by the wine in his old, confused brain.

" Taking his glass from the table, he held it away from him to scrutinise the colour ; thirsty as he was, it was not likely that he was going to drink trash ! Then, placing it to his lips, he took a sip.

' A very nice wine,' he said at last, passing it before his nose ; ' not the equal of my Heidsieck.'

It was at this moment that the idea came to him which he afterwards imparted at Timothy's in this nutshell : ' I shouldn't wonder a bit if that architect chap were sweet upon Mrs. Soames ! '

And from this moment his pale, round eyes never ceased to bulge with the interest of his discovery.

' The fellow,' he said to Mrs. Septimus, ' follows her about with his eyes like a dog—the bumpy beggar ! I don't wonder at it—she's a very charming woman, and I should say, the pink of discretion ! ' A vague consciousness of perfume clinging about Irene, like that from a flower with half-closed petals and a passionate heart, moved him to the creation of this image. ' But I wasn't sure of it,' he said, ' till I saw him pick up her handkerchief.' . . .

' Did he give it her back ? ' asked Mrs. Small.

' Give it back ? ' said Swithin, ' I saw him slobber on it when he thought I wasn't looking ! . . . But *she* gave him no encouragement,' went on Swithin ; he stopped, and stared for a minute or two in the way that so alarmed Aunt Hester—he had suddenly recollected that, as they were starting back in the phaeton, she had given Bosinney her hand a second time, and let it stay there, too. . . . He had touched his horses smartly with the whip, anxious to get her all to himself. But she had looked back, and she had not answered his first question ; neither had he been able to see her face—she had kept it hanging down."

An incident on the way forces from Irene's silent lips an amazing exclamation, in which the depth and intensity of the dream she is bringing back from Robin Hill are suddenly revealed.

"When, warmed by champagne, he had her all to himself, he unbosomed himself of his wrongs ; of his smothered resentment against the new *chef* at the Club . . . of his deafness, and that pain he sometimes got in his right side. She listened, her eyes swimming under their lids. He thought she was thinking deeply of his troubles, and pitied himself terribly. Yet in his fur coat, with frogs across the breast, his top hat aslant, driving this beautiful woman, he had never felt more distinguished."

He sits up accordingly with such an air of majesty that a costermonger, taking his girl for an airing, drives abreast of the phaeton in his donkey cart and begins to mimic him. Swithin realises that he is being guyed. His yellow, puffy face grows red ; he raises his whip to lash the insolent fellow ; the phaeton and the cart collide, and the dappled grays take fright.

" Swithin's great arms, stretched at full length, tugged at the reins. His cheeks were puffed, his lips compressed, his swollen face was of a dull, angry red. Irene had her hand on the rail, and at every lurch she gripped it tightly. Swithin heard her ask :

Are we going to have an accident, Uncle Swithin ?

He gasped out between his pants : ' It's nothing—
a little fresh.'

' I've never been in an accident.'

' Don't you move ! '   He took a look at her.   She
was smiling, perfectly calm.   ' Sit still,' he repeated.
' Never fear, I'll get you home.'

And in the midst of all his terrible efforts he was
surprised to hear her answer in a voice not like her
own :

' *I don't care if I never get home !* '

The carriage giving a terrible lurch, Swithin's exclamation was jerked back into his throat.   The horses,
winded by the rise of a hill, now steadied to a trot,
and finally stopped of their own accord.

' When '—Swithin described it at Timothy's—' I
pulled 'em up, there she was as cool as myself.   God
bless my soul !   She behaved as if she didn't care
whether she broke her neck or not.   What was it she
said, " I don't care if I never get home." '   Leaning
over the handle of his cane, he wheezed out, to Mrs.
Small's terror : ' And I'm not altogether surprised, with
a finicking feller like young Soames for a husband.' "

Now you know Swithin elementary and untutored.
He has shown himself in all his aspects.   You have
seen the old man, lapsing into senile torpor, the Englishman, grim and silent in the presence of danger.   In this
arrogant and rugged being you recognise what Mr.
Galsworthy has studied in all his novels : the national
and fundamental element which, either pure, or
weakened and refined by modern influences, is to be
found in all the Forsytes.

At the same time, something of the drama outside
him has been reflected in his staring, glassy eyes—a

ENGLISH LITERATURE

broken, distorted image which you are able to interpret for yourself, and the effect upon you is newer, truer, and more pathetic than if the scene between Irene and Bosinney were given to you directly. Newer, because the words of love are eternal, and we know them beforehand; truer, because thus it is that in the actual world the romance of a soul appears, not isolated and detached, but enclosed in all the indifferent life around it, merged in this life, and manifested only by brief indications here and there; more moving, because of the contrast between trivial realities, and the strange intermittent flashes which suggest the presence and the movements of passion in this everyday world.

Some of these flashes have a lightning quality. All you have as yet only half seen and guessed at becomes evident and definite in the light of such an utterance as that of Irene's, which startled even Uncle Swithin: "*I don't care if I never get home.*" You can now measure the advance the lovers have made towards each other, and you know that henceforth they can belong only to each other. That strange cry of Irene's, wrung from her by a physical shock, the sudden realisation of danger at a moment when Swithin's words, "I'll get you home"—that is to say, "to your husband"—have pierced to the point where her sensibilities concentrate, that cry brings out all that lay brooding under her silence, and what we now see is a soul possessed and desperate, for whom life contains henceforth nothing but a single image, and whose rapture makes it indifferent to the danger of death.

188

JOHN GALSWORTHY

Mr. Galsworthy's work abounds in such abrupt foreshortenings, which recall those of Balzac and Kipling, and bear witness to his creative and intuitive faculty as well as to his astonishing powers of analysis and perception. His characters are born of a large number of ideas and accumulated observations ; they gradually detach themselves from him ; henceforth, he has only to watch them living, and the details of their lives are so linked together by the logic of nature that their every word, act, passing expression, postulate and recall their past, their surroundings, habits and temperament—and beyond these, the more general and soul-stirring truths, the psychology of passion, sex and type, the hidden depths of man and of life.

The love story follows its secret course, coming up to the surface thus from time to time, and showing the two tragic figures ever more fervid, pale and solitary, predestined victims, because they are defying rigorous social conventions. Each time they are presented in a different aspect, according to the character through whom they are shown, and whose own nature is illuminated as it refracts the rising flame of their passion. The image of Irene which passed through Swithin's eyes was slight and colourless. Her beauty and her charm are brought home to us vividly through the vision of Jolyon the younger, a painter. He has the seeing eye and the understanding heart, for he himself has felt the dangerous Power that puts a strange light in a woman's face to paralyse the will of a man and subdue it to its own ends. He himself had travelled the mournful road " those two " were setting out upon ; he had disobeyed the law, he had foregone his caste, had stepped out of the ranks. He knew the solitude that awaited them. He observes the unknown lady with sympathetic interest and attention. The scene takes place in a corner of the Botanical Gardens where Irene, seated on a bench, is waiting for Bosinney. Young Jolyon is making a sketch there when he notices her ; he has never seen her before ; she is just a passing figure, but in this figure he at once feels the presence and emanation of passion.

" He saw a rounded chin nestling in a cream ruffle, a delicate face with large dark eyes and soft lips. A black ' picture ' hat concealed the hair ; her figure was lightly poised against the back of the bench, her knees were crossed ; the tip of a patent leather shoe emerged beneath her skirt. But Jolyon's attention was chiefly riveted by the look on her face, which reminded him of his wife. It was as though its owner had come into contact with forces too strong for her. It troubled him, rousing vague feelings of attraction and chivalry. Who was she ? And what doing there, alone ?

Two young men . . . came by on their way to lawn-tennis, and he noted with disapproval their furtive stares of admiration. A loitering gardener halted to do something unnecessary to a clump of pampas grass. . . . An old gentleman passed three times to scrutinise her long and stealthily, a queer expression about his lips.

With all these men young Jolyon felt the same vague irritation. She looked at none of them, yet was he certain that every man who passed would look at her like that.

Her face was not the face of a sorceress, who in every

look holds out to men the offer of pleasure ; it had none of the ' devil's beauty ' so highly prized among the first Forsytes of the land ; neither was it of that type, no less adorable, associated with the box of chocolate ; it was not of the spiritually passionate or the passionately spiritual order peculiar to house decoration and modern poetry ; nor did it seem to offer to the playwright material for the production of the interesting and neurasthenic figure, who commits suicide in the last act.

In shape and colouring, in its soft persuasive passivity, its sensuous purity, this woman's face reminded him of Titian's ' Heavenly Love.' And her attraction seemed to be in this soft passivity, in the feeling she gave that to pressure she must yield.

For whom was she waiting in the silence, with the trees dropping here and there a leaf, and the thrushes strutting close on grass touched with the sparkle of the autumn rime ?

Then her charming face grew eager, and glancing round with almost a lover's jealousy, young Jolyon saw Bosinney striding across the grass. . . They sat down close together, linked for all their outward discretion. He heard the rapid murmur of their talk, but what they said he could not catch.

He had rowed in that galley himself. He knew the long hours of waiting and the lean minutes of a half public meeting ; the tortures of suspense that haunt the unhallowed lover.

It required, however, but a glance at their two faces to see that this was none of those affairs of a season that distract men and women about town ; none of those sudden appetites that wake up ravening and are surfeited and asleep again in six weeks. This was the real thing. This was what had happened to himself ! Out of this anything might come !

Bosinney was pleading, and she so quiet, so soft,

yet immovable in her passivity, sat looking over the grass.

Was he the man to carry her off, that tender, passive being, who would never stir a step for herself ? Who had given him all herself, and would die for him, but perhaps would never run away with him !

It seemed to young Jolyon that he could hear her saying : ' But, darling, it would ruin you ! ' For he himself had experienced to the full the gnawing fear at the bottom of a woman's heart that she is a drag on the man she loves.

Gradually their talk ceased ; long silence followed.

' And where does Soames come in ? ' young Jolyon thought. ' People think she is concerned about the sin of deceiving her husband. Little they know of women ! She's eating after starvation—taking her revenge. And Heaven help her—for he'll take his.'

He heard a swish of silk, and spying round the laurel, saw them walking away, their hands stealthily joined. . . ."

Of course, you understand that when this meeting takes place Irene is already Bosinney's mistress. But let us see how this knowledge has come to us. Soames has quarrelled with his architect. He is bringing an action against him, an action that will inevitably ruin the imprudent artist, guilty, out of love for his work, of having exceeded his estimates for the house by the sum of three hundred and fifty pounds. " You are even meaner than I thought," says his wife turning from him when he announces this fact with his accustomed laconic hauteur. It is for us to imagine, from the following scene, which takes place a few days later, Irene's desperate reaction to the blow her husband has dealt the man she loves.

Soames is standing alone at the dining-room window. He is listening to a barrel organ playing a waltz, the waltz they had played at Roger's, and the perfume of the gardenias Irene had worn that evening comes back to him as it had drifted to him then, when she had passed, so pale and rapt, her eyes so soft, her lips parted, drawing Bosinney on and on in the maze of an endless dance.

" He turned, took a cigarette from the carven box, and walked back to the window. The tune had mesmerized him, and there came into his view Irene, her sunshade furled, hastening homewards down the square in a soft, rose-coloured blouse with drooping sleeves that he did not know. She stopped before the organ, took out her purse, and gave the woman money.

Soames shrank back, and stood where he could see into the hall.

She came in with her latch key, put down her sunshade, and stood looking at herself in the glass. Her cheeks were flushed as if the sun had burnt them ; her lips were parted in a smile. She stretched her arms out as though to embrace herself, with a laugh that for all the world was like a sob.

Soames stepped forward.

' Very—pretty ! ' he said.

But as though shot she spun round, and would have passed him up the stairs. He barred the way.

' Why such a hurry ? ' he said, and his eyes fastened on a curl of hair fallen loose across her ear.

He hardly recognised her. She seemed on fire, so deep and rich the colour of her cheeks, her eyes, her lips, and of the unusual blouse she wore.

She put up her hand and smoothed back the curl. She was breathing fast and deep, as though she had been running, and with every breath perfume seemed to come from her hair and from her body, like perfume from an opening flower.

' I don't like that blouse,' he said slowly, ' it's a soft, shapeless thing.'

He lifted his finger towards her breast, but she dashed his hand aside.

' Don't touch me ! ' she cried.

He caught her wrist ; she wrenched it away.

' And where may you have been ? ' he asked.

' In heaven—out of this house ! ' . . .

Outside, in thanksgiving, at the very door, the organ-grinder was playing the waltz."

I know not if Irene's words and looks have enlightened the haughty, unimaginative Soames as to the extent of his misfortune. The reader has understood, and does not wonder that with this dialogue the author brings one of the main divisions of his narrative to an end.

* * *

We now see how deliberately the author of *The Man of Property* relies upon omission and reticence. But we see, too, that the omissions are but apparent. All that Mr. Galsworthy does not tell us is implied in what he tells us ; hence the value of his brief notations. Each one records some tiny significant fact which brings to light important features of situation or character. The idea that governs his art is that the inner life of a man is seen only in flashes, that we never get a direct view of it—therefore that no direct description of it can be true—and further, that a character is part of an ever-moving group, where no single figure appears for a moment in the foreground without being eclipsed by others—therefore that it should not be kept too long before the footlights, and studied separately. In more general terms, the idea would seem to be that life, especially the life of the mind, is not transposable into terms of language, and that the logical association of words and phrases does not correspond to what is at once complete and fragmentary, fluid and solid, simple and complex in each moment of thought and feeling. Meredith had already declared that a single line was enough to describe a landscape—if one could find it. He meant, no doubt, that the novelist is less concerned to paint the landscape than to suggest it, less concerned to note its details than to convey an impression—the impression received by a certain character in the story, which would vary according to the psychology of the character, and, still more, according to the degree of intensity of his mood or action at the given moment. How much truer this is when, instead of dealing with forms and colours, the writer attempts to translate the life of a soul in all its fleeting variety—a life (simple though it be) so rich in shifting gradations. Here words would define what nature leaves shapeless, would fix that which is yet to be. There is but one method, one of which M. Bergson would approve : to call forth the reader's imagination, inciting him to fill in the gaps, and himself introduce the element of duration, that spiritual flux which cannot be perceived—in short, to convey to him the hidden life of the character. For though the writer may note the successive moments of that life, and mark the line of its course, he cannot reproduce its essence, which is a force in movement, a power passing into an act.[1]

IV

We must also remember that if emotion and passion are essentially internal, this is peculiarly the case in northern countries, where the reactions of the nerves, and their discharge by speech and gesture are slower and less frequent than elsewhere—especially in England, where the chief aim of education is the training of the will, and the peculiar social discipline teaches a man to curb his impulses, and not to " give himself away." A Soames Forsyte is by nature no less vulgar and snobbish than his father ; but he has been a pupil of aristocratic Eton, and he is taciturn because he thinks it beneath his social dignity to unbosom himself. This English reticence is a mixture of contempt, shyness and modesty, but above all, of that

---

[1] The passage above has been translated into English as follows by M. Bergson himself (*see Prefatory Note*) :

" Words would bring the shapeless to a definite shape, and crystallise into *being* what is only *becoming*. Only one method will avail, and M. Bergson would approve of it ; we must call forth a sympathetic intuition, and induce the reader to fill up the gaps with his own imagination, thus leaving him to introduce the element of pure duration or spiritual flux which we are unable to supply. In fact, he must be made to bring on within himself the flow of feeling which we wish him to realise. Of this inner movement the writer can only note, one after the other, the stationary moments. He designs its track, but he cannot give out its essence, which is a force at work, the potential developing into the real."

profound instinct for the conditions of health which is
widespread in England. The English feel that sensibility is akin to weakness, is almost a preliminary
stage of disease—disease which must not be propa-
gated; they feel that emotion disturbs the mental
balance and attacks those powers of certitude and
decision which make for unity and resistance—what
they call *character*, and prize above all things. When
some sudden shock unseals their lips and wrings an
expression of deep feeling from them, they seem at
once alarmed and ashamed, as if they had confessed
weakness and inferiority, or been guilty of a solecism,
a derogation from the ideal held up to them from their
school-days, recognised and imposed by opinion : the
English ideal proper, not of intelligence, but of will.
This trait is so essentially a caste characteristic that
Mr. Galsworthy, who never ceases to study the English
gentry, has often made it a special theme—certain
short stories and certain chapters in his novels were
written solely to illustrate it.[1] In general, he merely
notes the passing evidences of it ; he excels in making
mere silence, an arrested movement, as significant as
decisive action. In *The Patrician*, for instance, where
we see Lord Valleys, that consummate type of the
English aristocrat, in conflict with his son, Lord Miltoun,
no less haughtily self-contained and disciplined than
himself, and even more determined, because more
passionate, the trait is sufficiently indicated by even

---

[1] *The Japanese Quince* in *A Motley*, also the chapter of
Mrs. Pendyce's Return in *The Country House*, and that called
English in *The Island Pharisees*.

less than a gesture, by the mere suppression of a gesture, in the course of an apparently ordinary conversation where two strong wills are confronted.

" Thus spasmodically the conversation ran till the last servant had left the room.

Then Miltoun, without any preparation, looked straight at his father and said :

' I mean to marry Mrs. Noel, sir.'

Lord Valleys received the shock with exactly the same expression as that with which he was accustomed to watch his horses beaten. Then he raised his wine-glass to his lips, and set it down again untouched. This was the only sign he gave of interest or discomfiture.

' Isn't this rather sudden ? ' . . .

. . . Suddenly Miltoun noticed that a wafer in Lord Valleys' hand was quivering. This brought into his eyes no look of compunction, but such a smouldering gaze as the old Tudor Churchman might have bent on an adversary who showed a sign of weakness. Lord Valleys, too, noticed the quivering of that wafer and ate it."

Stendhal recognised the type of human energy only in the agitations and dangerous outbursts of his passionate Italians. An energy superior to that of passion is concentrated in these disciplined English —the energy of will. But the ardour and the conflict of the two is suggested by almost imperceptible signs —the fire of a glance, the slight trembling of a hand. Thus, when two electric currents meet, the short crackling sounds, the sudden flash of angry sparks, reveal the presence of the fluid and intimate its strength and tension.

JOHN GALSWORTHY

For in these souls the forces of desire and dream are vehement, all the more so because, instead of spending themselves at once, they accumulate until, under some sudden shock, they break into tragic explosion or perhaps lyrical outpourings. As a rule Mr. Galsworthy, a painter of types and manners, deals chiefly with average characters. But they are English, capable of intense secret passion, however trivial and vulgar the object of this passion. When you know Horace Pendyce, the country squire, George Pendyce, the clubman, Bianca Dallison, the woman of the world, such a merchant, such a business man, such a lawyer as Jolyon, James and Soames Forsyte, people whose conversation in real life would make you yawn in ten minutes, you understand the reserves of passion and of will people of this class may conceal beneath their ordinary and gregarious aspects, obedient though they be to their conventions. You realise their capacity for love, hate, greed, resentment, suspicion, pride, obstinacy and self-assertion, and recognise the deep hidden energies that nourish their lonely, jealous and irreducible souls.

V

Here we have that " hypertrophy of the *ego* " which Taine pronounced to be the main characteristic of the English. It would seem that in this island of grayness and mist, where objects are seen as it were through a veil, where the life of nature is slow and hardly perceptible, where everything bears the trace of human effort, the inner life of the soul has developed to excess. It would seem that will and feeling, which constitute a man's individual character and energy, take precedence of intelligence and sensation, the less personal elements, through which the order and diversity of the world are reflected in him. This *ego* the Englishman projects upon his world, and his vision of the universe is distorted by his special tendencies ; he is interested in it only so far as it can be adapted to his own ends, or made to yield .nourishment· for his intimate stock of beliefs, sentiments and aspirations. Self-contained and introspective, his inner life is his main object. Hence his absorption in spiritual realities. Hence his religion, which is less a ritual system, bound up with a certain dogmatic explanation of the universe than an appeal to conscience, and, as Matthew Arnold said, morality touched with a certain emotion—a feeling for what is sacred. Hence his art, which overlays the real with the colours of his own dream, and is addressed rather to the soul than to the senses, seeking in the visible world signs of the invisible, lessons, symbols, and moving suggestions. Hence finally, his essentially psychological and moralistic literature, intent now on the fervent teaching of an idea, now on a meditation on life, now on the expression of the lyrical or the pathetic, but always on an infinite study of souls, of their deep and more or less lonely life, their slow developments and their crises.

From an early date the efforts of English novelists have all tended in this direction, and Henry James, Arnold Bennett and John Galsworthy have continued the tradition. In France, art, as represented by

JOHN GALSWORTHY

Gautier, Flaubert, the Goncourts, Alphonse Daudet, Huysmans, and Loti strove to render sensations either strongly or delicately, to seize the unique element in the appearance of each object by a choice and arrangement of words conveying at the same time impressions of rhythm, rare, simple or complex beauty, as in painting a tone, and in music a harmony are precious by reason of their essential quality and position, irrespective of their significance. The English, on the other hand, exerted themselves more and more to penetrate, analyse and translate the inner life of the human creature. They burrowed more deeply into it than our psychological novelists, for they were not content, as were often Stendhal and his school, to follow, in the self-analysis of their characters, developments and involutions of thought, associations of ideas which, like the monologues of Racine, originate in the conscious activities of the brain. They penetrated the chiaroscuro, the dark depths, where feeling and volition are born. They sought to seize and render the actual person, its special tones and rhythms, to communicate the incommunicable, that which distinguishes it from all others, and so constitutes it a person. They followed the slow evolution of a mind showing its latent forces in the daily round before displaying them in the drama. They did not, like Stendhal, overlook the physical man, the visible form evolved by the same energies that develop the soul and direct its movement : a revealing form, gradually impressed upon matter by the process of life. Outside of the individual, they examined all that relates to him, and first of all, everything that expresses him, his dwelling, the familiar accessories that proclaim his tastes and habits, and harmonise with the living being from whom they derive; and then the things that influence him, his social and natural surroundings, the landscape about him—studied, not for its own sake, not for its independent beauty as a pure artistic theme, but in its relation to the character, its suggestions of mood and feeling, its correspondence with types, habits and ideas.

This keen interest of English novelists in the moral world was accompanied by special technical research. They were eager to translate what they discovered, and they never ceased to make discoveries, their sensibility to psychological facts becoming keener as they observed. They were eager to extend and refine their art, to superimpose it, detail by detail and shade by shade, on spiritual reality, each moment, each particle of which was revealed to them ever richer and more complex. They had begun by merely relating and commenting; they now combined description of spiritual states with the narrative. This study George Eliot carried further by introducing, together with the precision of scientific terminology, the methods of professional psychologists, and the ideas of philosophers, of determinists and Darwinians. Opposing the natural tendency of the individual to the pressure of his environment, she presented life as the resultant of these two forces. She discovered the secret principle of fate in the germ, and brought to light the imperceptible original taint that produces its effects of abortion or disaster only in the distant future. She showed man shaping himself day by day, each of his acts contributing something to his final form ; she followed out the generation and the development of this to the infinitesimal ; she observed the birth and elaboration of sentiments, the delicate detail of acts of volition, the imponderable influences which are added to the measurable weight of motives, the imperceptible trembling of the scale before the final and decisive movement, which she eventually judged, by a paradox not unusual among determinists, from the single point of view of a strict conscience. Yet such judgments, induced by the Puritan belief in the importance of acts, were tempered by the charity of a great soul, full of an intimate pity for human suffering, and sympathy with the pathos of humble lives.

It seemed impossible to carry this study of moral life further. But it was a study ; not exactly life. This life itself, its very flux, Meredith attempted to note, and this without explaining or analysing it, by placing himself in the centre of each of his characters, in order to show us the outer world, landscapes and events in the vision each one forms of them, and transmit to us the play of images and ideas which compose the mental activity of each—a complex, intermittent play, where thought at every moment mingles with feeling and sensation, moves simultaneously on several planes, halts and starts again in unforeseen directions. And, beneath, he reached the subconscious life, all those deeper strata of a soul where the traces of the past are registered, and whence arise reminiscences, impulses, the sudden gesture of instinct or habit. The uncertain murmurs of groping thought, the faintest quiver of the nerves, the slight and multiple vibrations that awaken like harmonics around a sensation or an idea, rippling and dying away in the depths of the unconscious, the unknown resonances which linger there and give the tonality of the soul; all this was made audible rather than described by Meredith. Such were the true subject and substance of those great novels, *The Egoist* and *One of our Conquerors*. The happenings in these are purely spiritual, or rather the events properly so-called, the changes of situation, the details of the action and its development are but the gradual outward manifestation of forces in characters at war with one another.

A new language, a new style, had to be invented to render this shifting life, its fleeting shades, sudden changes, meanderings and recoils, the minute, incessant actions and reactions of which it is made up—an art that would translate what the characters themselves cannot translate, the imperceptible germination of idea and sentiment, movements dimly astir in the depths of the mind. Of all these intangibles, Meredith manages to convey to us a direct sensation by indirect means—methods which, as his best critic has said, " are in strong contrast to the French ideal of the unique word," that crystal which fails to fix all the restless fluidity of the spirit. This infinite life of the soul for which there are no words he has suggested by means of swift images, broken or confused, analogies, and brief allusions. By a variety of devices, he has rendered the fugitive and instantaneous character of this life, in which sensation, feeling and ideas intermingle. This he has done chiefly by suggestive foreshortenings, by the use of those compound words which the genius of the English language admits, words in which the verb and the adverb, the noun and the adjective combine to express things the French tongue dissociates logically : the action and its circumstances, the object and its moments ; and further, by ellipses and preteritions, by sudden gaps in the dialogue, which he expects the reader to bridge for himself. Thus, he adapts his image of life to the speed of " our flying minds," whose perceptions outrun descriptions and analyses. By this method the author of *The Egoist* has achieved incomparable results.[1]

[1] The four lines immediately following are M. Bergson's own translation into English of the text (*see Prefatory Note*) :
" The French language expresses mainly forms, clean-cut sections forced into reality by analysis—in fact, the ready-made. It is far easier to render in English what Monsieur Bergson calls ' the being made ' (*le se faisant*)," the process which it has been his triumph as a writer to have defined in a general manner, in despite of the customs and tendencies of the language. To illustrate this point a practically untranslatable passage from Meredith's *One of our Conquerors* may be taken. It will show to what depths, to what physiological roots of the human being, the great English novelist penetrates, laying bare the secret workings by which the carnal, elementary sap is finally transmuted into the loftiest spiritual blossom. Young Nesta Radnor, a creature of pure, intense vitality, intuitively discovering life, has just made her spiritual choice of Dartrey Fenellan, whom she eventually marries. At this moment in the story she is walking with her father, whom she adores, and who is talking to her.
" At times he touched deep in humaneness ; and he set

The danger was obscurity, and we know that Meredith is considered obscure. He was so to his contemporaries and compatriots; he will be much more so to future English generations, and, like Browning, he is almost inaccessible to foreigners. The reason is that suggestive allusion and analogy, the oblique image which by reflection is to light up the imperceptible, appeal only to those who live at the same period and in the same surroundings as the writer. We must be at one with him in our mental habits, our instinctive associations, if by such indirect means, he is to awake in us certain echoes, and stir the chords which he is either unwilling to strike directly or which are unresponsive when so struck. In any case, it would seem that alone the inventor of an art so difficult and delicate

her heart leaping on the flash of a thought to lay it bare with the secret it held, for his help. That was a dream. She could more easily have uttered the words to Captain Dartrey, after her remembered abashing holy tremor of the vision of doing it and casting herself on noblest man's compassionateness; and her imagined thousand emotions —a rolling music within her, a wreath of cloud glory in her sky—which had, as with virgins it may, *plighted her body to him for sheer urgency of soul; drawn her by a single unwitting-to-brain, unconscious-in-blood, shy curl outward of the sheathing leaf to the flowering of woman to him; even to the shore of that strange sea, where the maid stands choosing this one man for her destiny, as in a trance. So are those young ones unfolded, shade by shade; and a shade is all the difference with them; they can teach the poet to marvel at the immensity of vitality in ' the shadow of a shade.'* " (*One of our Conquerors*, Chapter XXXVI.)

[The italics in the most characteristic lines of the passage are ours.]

can wield all its magic. The writer who attempts to note every vibration of the soul seems tedious as soon as we miss the miraculous effect of instantaneous transmission. This was brought home to Mr. Henry James, whose work contains wonders of psychological subtlety and skill, when he changed his manner for one akin to that of Meredith. When we read a story like *The Velvet Glove* we are not reminded of the best pages of *The Egoist,* but of that famous and formidable first chapter of *One of our Conquerors,* which records all the nascent, intermingled, repercussant waves of sensation started, by a fall on London Bridge, in the brain of Victor Radnor, the sprightly gentleman in a white waistcoat who does not reach the other end of the bridge till the end of the twentieth page.

In this development of the English novel, Mr. Galsworthy's contribution is both new and important. He, too, is interested in the obscure fibres and delicate movements of the soul. O his gift of swift, subtle observation we chose our examples mainly from the history of the Forsytes. This was because the Forsytes are comparatively simple. When Mr. Galsworthy deals with types of a higher culture, artists, writers, dreamers, the Shelton of *The Island Pharisees,* the Dallisons of *Fraternity,* people so remote, so critical, so full of delicate and hidden sensibility, his art becomes so complex, the work is so cunningly woven, made up of so many minute complementary touches and secret reminiscences, that it is impossible to study it in detail. Hardly any incidents are recorded. As in real life the lapse of time alone, the succession of minutes and days, seem to change the position of the characters imperceptibly. One might say that the magnitude of the dynamic forces, the line described by the principal characters in the course of the novel are here presented to us by a process which is an aggregation of the infinitesimal. Add to this that self-consciousness, pride, obedience to the rules of caste, do not let the characters express themselves—for instance, Bianca Dallison, the proud rather than jealous wife, and Hilary Dallison, who, though he will not admit it even to himself, is fascinated by a little daughter of the people, do not allow themselves any manifestation of feeling. Consider, too, that this reticent couple, paralysed by their habits of doubt and introspection, and fettered by their respect for convention, act but negatively, ever withdrawing, shrinking, repressing, and trying to escape responsibility. The strange thing in the conjugal drama which forms the subject of *Fraternity* is that from beginning to end it remains mute and invisible. The final and inevitable crisis is brought about by the gradual accumulation of minute circumstances, by the petty daily play of characteristic impressions and reactions of the soul. There is no scene of any sort between husband and wife. Without any apparent shock or conflict, a rift appears in their relations, and widens slowly and surely. The drama closes naturally with the quiet exit of the husband. The secret process suggested here makes one think of those imperceptible molecular activities which culminate in the silent, spontaneous rupture of an impossible fusion of metals. How the structure and the intimate movement of souls is revealed in such a study ! We seem to be looking at them through a magnifying glass, or, rather, listening through a microphone to their life-breath. Their slightest vibrations acquire an unexpected value, and meaning ; their very silences are full of strange, disturbing murmurs, significant of the inner being.

All this recalls *The Egoist*, and would recall it still more if the characters spoke more. We cannot read these novels of detached ironic observation without thinking of Meredith. Not only is Mr. Galsworthy's object the same—the study of psychological life on all planes of the soul—not only is his art analogous, hinting, suggesting, but we find in it much of the master's philosophy. There is the same criticism of " Pharisaic " England, the same denunciation of masculine selfishness and the tyranny it exercises over women, the same fundamental idealism. But we seem also to trace something of Turgenev's influence, clarifying, relieving and moderating the whole. Such an art, however rooted in sentiment, is entirely governed by the intellect. It is more lucid, more conscious, and in general more perfect than that of Meredith, but for this very reason less vivid and impetuous, less inevitable, less full of that primitive, ethnic vitality, which alternately delights and disconcerts us in the creator of Richard Feverel and Nevil Beauchamp : his Shakespearean fantasy, the inspired dance of his imagination, now a mad jig tearing asunder the web of his work, now a sudden flight that carries him soaring to the empyrean.

Mr. Galsworthy, moreover, has been careful to

borrow nothing from Meredith's dangerous and over-metaphorical style. His own is admirably limpid. Even if we do not take in the whole of his thought at first, we are never conscious of not understanding. In the structure of such a novel as *Fraternity*, several planes are superposed. If we are inattentive, if our observation is superficial, we see but the nearest and most material, on which the characters move and speak. Here we have the ordinary appearances of reality ; they evolve with the natural logic of life. It is merely life going on before us, the more recognisable and intelligible in that our powers of vision are limited.

But if our eyes gradually become keener, if we begin to observe and interpret, other planes will appear, intersecting or succeeding one another—that, for instance, where, almost invisibly, certain incidents take place, certain figures live, which influence the leading characters—or, most important of all, that plane where the deeper psychological life is stirring, which we see projected on the clear surface of the novel in acts, speech and events. And beneath these manifold strata, on a plane which upholds all the rest, we have the author's personal thought, the secret intention, of which his story, under ordinary forms, presents symbols alone. The first reading of *Fraternity* delighted me ; yet it was not until the second that I saw the general and hidden idea of the book, all its intimate and mystic meaning, implied on the first page in the description of a sunset cloud. It is almost impossible to grasp the pantheistic intention of this passage if one has not already felt the main suggestions of the work. But there is no difficulty, no sense of mystery : we have but a picture of a sky such as many novelists paint. Nearly all Mr. Galsworthy's landscapes contain veiled meanings of the same sort, prolonging and completing the philosophical idea he refrains from expressing, because he prefers to leave it indistinct and multiple, rich in possibilities we can only guess at. The nature he thus evokes is pantheistic, permeated by a vague general life in which everything moves collectively. By these fleeting images of earth and sky he makes us feel the divine at work in the heart of things, the obscure will that develops the universe, the unique, hidden reality in which every being has its substance—and in this brief vision, the values of the tiny individuals who call themselves " *I*," and see nothing but their own affairs in the world, are changed ; their history takes on a new meaning, ironic or pathetic.

Often a more special idea is interwoven in these landscapes. If there be indeed a soul in Nature, something akin to the deep, elemental states of our own souls may pass into it. There may be a correspondence between a certain aspect of a thing, and some passion or emotion that stirs a character in the novel. Generally, when Mr. Galsworthy describes, he does so to suggest something he has not told us about a person. Such, for instance, was his object in the admirable picture of an evening at Richmond in *The Man of Property*. Irene and Bosinney, drawn to each other, but unable to speak because they are not alone, are bathed in an ecstatic June twilight, a blue dimness, heavy with the scent of the flower-laden lime trees, an affluence of

saps and perfumes, a languor emanating from an
unusual mood of Nature. All this, which on such a
day vaguely disturbs the most positive of the Forsytes,
tells us, without any insistence on the author's part,
that the Power as old as the world is at work in poor
Irene, permeating, transfiguring and enfolding her,
changing her into a flower—a human flower, perfumed
like those the spring has brought out once more in
thousands on the old trees, whose destiny is accomplished when they have lived their brief hour of love
and beauty.

Sometimes the reminder of the great realities is
briefer and still more mysterious. It may be a sudden,
unexplained impression received by one of the characters, accompanied by a vague, rapid intuition we are
left to imagine, which opens an abyss before him :
a sudden vision, the memory of which recurs from
time to time, changing his attitude and his idea of
life for a moment. Thus Soames, the man of property,
the impassive, overbearing husband of Irene, shudders
in the night at the mournful, voluptuous cry of a peacock, no doubt because he hears in it the call of desire,
of Love, elemental, mysterious and strong as Nature,
surrounding and haunting his house, threatening his
pride and his security. Thus Hilary, the sad and
delicate sceptic, the detached dreamer, leaning out of
his window at two o'clock in the morning in London,
hears in the nocturnal silence a dull sound, swelling
and nearing, till it seems an immense thunderous
roar, rising from the whole city. It is only the
noise of hundreds of carts coming in from the country

to the markets, but it frightens him and sets his heart beating—may be because, to this sensitive dilettante holding aloof from life, it is the noise of life astir in the darkness, of the immeasurable, inevitable life beating around his solitude, laden with the suffering and effort of man. Something inexpressible is obscurely revealed to him at this moment, the fugitive and tremulous memory of which will recur to him later, throwing him back into his trance.

Other symbols are more definite. Side by side with the principal characters, we have a series of secondary figures in which the same idea is incarnated or suggested. For instance—in *Fraternity* again—the pauper family whose acts and mutual relations re-echo, at each moment of the narrative something of the Dallisons' story, so that the same unchanging humanity reveals itself among these well-to-do people and these outcasts ; through all the difference of class, the last appear to us as shadows of the first—their mournful shadows projected on the plane of poverty. Sometimes it is just an animal which follows its master, bearing the mark of his ownership, and somehow resembling him. Thus in *The Country House* Horace Pendyce's spaniel—a type of the submission and mute adoration this worthy squire unconsciously exacts from those about him, because twenty generations of petty rural potentates have transmitted to him their habits and domineering instincts. Thus again in *Fraternity*, in attendance on Hilary Dallison—a writer in whom culture has killed nature, now an infirm soul, emptied of will, given over to brooding sensibility—there is the pale little bull-dog, with instincts almost as dead as those of his master—no less town-bred, civilised, intelligent, and assured of his daily meal ; an admirable creature, fond of solitude and silence by the library door, quite independent of his own kind, but suddenly arrested one day in Hyde Park before a dog still more extraordinary than himself, a white, curly poodle, motionless, odourless, round which he walks with an air of stupefied admiration, as if he had at last found the ideal dog, the perfect and definitive product of civilisation in the canine race. Indeed, there is nothing of nature left in this animal ; it has reached the highest stage of artificiality—a cardboard poodle. But such images are mere echoes of ideas, and the effect cannot be suggested by examples. Pointing out one of these analogies to the reader entails an explanation. The two terms which the author had kept separate are juxtaposed, whereas one alone should at once call up the other. The swift, fleeting allusion becomes heavy —a deliberate metaphor—and the symbol develops into a parable.

The art of this writer as a whole is a very novel effort to penetrate to the heart of life, to seize and render its most fugitive aspects—those which cannot as a rule be transposed by art without being dissociated, sharply defined, and subjected to the simplicity of fixed forms. This he succeeds in doing by means apparently simple, but in reality extraordinarily subtle. The chief of these is the calculated choice, the unobtrusive arrangement of characteristic detail. This device, to which we have already called attention, is the feature that strikes us first. Those details, minute and trivial when isolated—the manner in which the dreary James carries his umbrella, the decisive gesture with which the stern old Lady Casterley crushes a hornet—contribute to our understanding of a certain nature, to our vision of a certain temperament. For Mr. Galsworthy combines insight into psychologic life with a keen perception of all that expresses it outwardly. Hence, the aesthetic value of the infinitesimal phenomena which another writer would not have thought of interpreting, or would have neglected as useless. They serve in his hands to enlarge the domain of art, to introduce more elements and expressions of life, to seize reality more firmly and so make it appear richer and more interesting. We find in his work an advance in technique and sensibility akin to that which among contemporary painters and sculptors responds to the demands of the modern eye. In a tone which seemed simple, in some relief of a living body we supposed smooth, they daily perceive and reveal to us more palpitating complexity. It is easy to go too far in this study of the element. But in the hands of great artists—and the author of *Fraternity* is one—the quiver and pulsation of the marble, the subtle modelling and all the play of sensitive shadows obey the direction of a fundamental line and idea.

There now remains what we have seen to be the most original factor in Mr. Galsworthy's art, one which he contrives to combine with all this wealth of detail : his refusal to say everything, his preference for subtle allusion, his skill in suggesting what he judges to be truer and more moving if left undefined. We have tried to examine this delicate device. But here we are baffled by that mysterious element we recognise in every fine work of art, and which defies analysis. After reading *Fraternity* we ask ourselves by what secret magic the figure of Hilary Dallison's wife, the haughty, distant, enigmatic and ironical Bianca, has become so real and haunting a presence to us. There is no description of her, no dissection of her soul, and half a page would contain all the words she utters in the two hundred pages of the novel—words deliberately inexpressive, and hence all the more expressive of her proud self-discipline and reticence, for one may say of her as of all the other Dallisons, of all the Forsytes, of all the Caradocs, of all the Dennants, what Mr. Galsworthy says of George Pendyce, and what is true of all the English governing class : " It was one of the articles of his faith that the expression of emotion is forbidden." Such again is the case in *The Man of Property*, with young Jolyon's wife and former mistress, who does not speak half a dozen words, whose name we do not know, whose face we see but once, when, raising her head, she colours under her father-in-law's scrutiny— a blush made all the more pathetic by her gray hair. How we guess at her painful past, at all the trembling anxiety and distrust it has bred in her, at her monotonous, stinted home-life, at her sensitive pride seeking refuge in solitude, at the jealous passion she concentrates on her husband ! And all this is suggested by two or three significant gestures the value of which

is enhanced by the situation. We must not, however, overlook the quick, many-tinted play of reflec-
tions between the characters, which show them to
us in each other, the brief flashes by which they are
mutually lit up—all that juggling with mirror-souls
which the author of *The Egoist* initiated.

The reader now sees more or less how Mr. Galsworthy
escapes the difficulty of Meredith's style, while probing
the soul no less deeply. If he recalls Meredith by
certain oblique methods of evocation, he is able to
dispense with those labyrinthine images used by the
master to translate the untranslatable things of the
spirit, and this by certain skilful hints and suggestions.
One reason is that his object is not the same. Save in
The Patrician—the last, and one of the most powerful,
but from the standpoint of technique, the least original
of this series (for Mr. Galsworthy has changed his
manner from volume to volume)—he does not paint
exceptional figures, lofty types like a Richard Feverel,
a Nevil Beauchamp, a Diana of the Crossways, a Lord
Ormont, or a Victor Radnor, to whom their creator has
lent something of his own incomparable vitality, his
winged spirit, given at times a touch of his own genius,
and communicated the glow of his own flame. Nor
does he deal with extraordinary cases like those of
Evan Harrington or Carinthia, with monstrosities like
the egoism of Sir Willoughby Patterne, the frenzied
pride of Fleetwood or the splendid charlatanism of
Roy Richmond. He does not magnify the scale of
nature. He depicts no epics of the soul. He studies
average types, samples of contemporary English society

and classes, figures therefore to which his public is accustomed, and which an English reader can imagine from slight touches. Behind the Forsytes, this reader will see the upper middle class townsfolk, the parvenus of the nineteenth century, conspicuous for their respect for money, their intolerance and snobbishness; behind the Pendyces, the old Tory gentry of the counties, the ancient caste, the despotic fox-hunting justices of the peace, patrons, from father to son, of the small rural population; behind the Dallisons, the world of intellectuals, refined and sensitised by culture, still obedient (an essentially English trait) in spite of their delicate, reticent scepticism, to codes of Puritan origin, but to whom the religious principle has become a social imperative; finally, behind the Caradocs, the aristocracy, trained by a stoic discipline to a proud worship of character, traditionally devoted to public affairs, but much freer in thought and action, much more independent of conventions and *cant* than the middle classes, and therefore more spontaneous, nearer to nature, more capable of understanding the impulsive and instinctive masses, and of being understood by them.

Mr. Galsworthy's singular art and talent had to be considered first. It would now remain to study these types, to consider how far they represent English ideas, those active ideas which fashioned them, and of which they are the living expression. This, perhaps, would be the best method of studying the England of to-day; it is all portrayed in the unfinished work of this great novelist. Further, we should have to show what satire underlies his work, what ideal is opposed therein to the ideas prevailing on the other side of the Channel, I mean those established ideas· perpetuated by tradition and hereditary prejudice, which have not ceased to govern morals and manners. We should then see what a secret passion of pity for suffering softens or sharpens his irony, what fervour of love inspires it all —what a mystic, almost Hindu sense of the divine unity of the world, where not only all human beings, but all perishable creatures are brethren, and of the same essence.

SHAKESPEARE AND THE ENGLISH SOUL [1]

ENGLAND has just commemorated the three hundredth anniversary of the death of Shakespeare with religious fervour. In the midst of the most terrible war in her history she has turned back to the shadowy and no doubt somewhat imaginary figure of the greatest of her sons, that Englishman of the Renaissance in whom the human spirit, in the course of its myriad incarnations, achieved one of its most glorious avatars. Of this man we know hardly anything, for his person has disappeared in his work; and like some strange sea-creature of which nothing remains but the marvel of an iridescent spiral, he has been transmuted into his own manifold creation. This almost complete eclipse of the individual counts, no doubt, for a good deal in the national worship of the poet. A hero is more easily deified when nothing remains of his human personality, and his work also becomes more unaccountable.

Shakespeare seems to have risen out of nothing—a strange, scattered music, mysteriously brought together in the English sky of the Renaissance, like those

---

[1] Written on the occasion of the Shakespeare tercentenary, April, 1916.

strains floating in the resonant azure of the magic isle
—that concert of invisible spirits led by the celestial
voice of Ariel. This music seems to soar from the
whole of the English soil. We hear it in the legendary
murmur of the past, the flutter of Celtic fairies and
will-o'-the-wisps, the undying voices of moor and wood-
land that endure through the days and nights of centuries, like the timeless ripple of streams in the hollows
—sounds which a Hardy has heard and made us hear
under the clangours of modern England, ever the same,
as if nothing in the world had changed since the
beginnings of that land. Thus, in Shakespeare, the
English recognise more or less clearly, behind the
creatures of his fancy, the ancient spirit of the English
soil. He has made them one for ever with the calm
landscapes of the past—broad acres, cottages thatched
and flower-wreathed, patriarchal oaks, green meadows
where spring is fresher and more splendid than elsewhere—landscapes that have survived here and there
in the south and south-west of the island, in the Strat-
ford country itself, and have become the cherished
image of the land since the changes that have made
England more and more industrial and urban. If,
severed from this atmosphere and this background, the
fateful figures created by his genius were isolated,
as are Michelangelo's superhuman marbles in the
dim silence of San Lorenzo, the poet's work would
not be national. To the Englishman of to-day,
Shakespeare is not only the greatest genius of the
English race. In him the whole genius of England is
expressed.

ENGLISH LITERATURE

I

How much truth is there in this belief ?

When, after a visit to modern England, we read Shakespeare again, our first impression is that he is altogether remote from it. His characters, and his own personality, as far as we can read it in his works, seem to be of a different species from the Englishman of to-day. I have in mind here not the Englishman as conceived by other nations (though he, indeed, is not purely imaginary), but the type our neighbours themselves consider national, a type their novelists describe either approvingly or critically, one obviously related to the figures painted by their predecessors. For we find it in the pictures of Meredith, George Eliot, Thackeray, and even, with certain shades of difference, in those of Dickens ; in those of Charlotte Brontë and Mrs. Gaskell it seems to be suggested. Defoe's Robinson Crusoe was an earlier rendering of the type, and Carlyle, who admired it so much, endowed it with the virtues he loved best : energy, untiring effort, acceptance of monotony, tenacity in conflict, taciturnity, a taste for solitude, strength and simplicity of conviction ; in a word : stability of the whole moral character.

Of such a type the fundamental trait is undoubtedly that which Taine had pointed out: the singular force of a soul supported by habits and beliefs, resisting influence from without, and finding its joy and plenitude in effort ; an effort turned inwards to shape oneself according to a preconceived ideal, and an effort working upon the outer world to subdue and utilise it.

In the language of the schools, one might say that what is here notable is the solidity of the psychic structure. The soul is firmly built up on fixed lines of feeling, belief and will, which secure it against the shocks of emotion ; hence its continuity of action, its steady hold upon things and strange impassibility. Such a soul, almost impervious to the pressure of the environment, almost incapable of intuitive sympathy, because so firmly fixed in its personal form, would be naturally prone to pride and egotism—the faults English novelists and moralists have criticised most frequently—were it not that the culture which has so enhanced its powers of resistance—a peculiarly English culture of Puritan origin—has also imposed upon it certain disciplinary ideas, directing its energies to ideal ends. Be the end what it may, ideal or material, personal or disinterested, the man thus constituted pursues it with unswerving will—a will which it is the constant aim of English education to fortify. His strength lies in his faithfulness : faithfulness to the enterprise on which he has entered, to the word he has pledged, faithfulness to himself, this law, his beliefs, his watchwords, which, whether selfish or altruistic, are generally accepted by him as moral duties.

It is the virile quality *par excellence ;* and when the Englishman compares himself, not only to certain foreign nations, but to other races within the United Kingdom, he justly conceives of himself as the masculine type. Consciousness of his own characteristics has increased with his knowledge of the diversity of the human race ; he has recognised how important and peculiar they are. Never has he studied himself so carefully as to-day. Kipling, in his Indian officers and Civil Servants, nearly all untouched by the influences of the Far East, Galsworthy in his Pendyces and Forsytes, Bennett in his Clayhanger, many others, have shown him in his different aspects, sometimes affectionately, sometimes with a satirical intention. But all alike have seen in him a distinct type of humanity, a variant of the species, set apart from the rest by the strength and fixity of his characteristics and his survival in an age of critical culture—all the more interesting, according to the English convictions of to-day, because, though other strains, the livelier and more sensitive Cymric and Gaelic, have contributed more largely to the arts, the poetry and the intellectual civilisation of Great Britain, it is he, the less brilliant partner, who, by his conscience, his endurance, his activity, his mute and commanding energy, all his positive and practical virtues, has built up the moral vigour and greatness of the Empire—of that Empire which Cecil Rhodes explained when he said that the world belongs to the unimaginative races.

The type is, of course, an ancient one. Since the time of Carlyle, who enriched the theme with many eloquent variations, it has been an axiom on the other side of the Channel that it is especially Anglo-Saxon, that the serf of the Norman conquest, the yeoman, and the citizen of the free English communes were its remote ancestors, that it was strengthened by the struggle, first for political, and then for religious liberty. It is to be recognised in certain robust figures of Chaucer's, in Langland's *Piers Plowman*, and may be imagined in a Wycliffe. But it did not manifest itself fully till the Reformation, and the Reformation not only revealed it, but made it more general and complete. Indeed, in its final modern form, it certainly appears as a product of culture, of biblical and religious culture, in which first the Decalogue, and then the moral law, become the essential element of religion. The Puritan discipline undoubtedly taught man self-reliance, developed his will-power, and ensured the stability of his person at the expense of spontaneity, by enjoining on the soul unceasing self-watchfulness to ensure obedience to the law, by training it to repress impulse and instinct, to resist fatigue or *ennui*, and do its duty to the end, remembering that it stands alone —alone responsible for its actions—that conduct is the first consideration in life. No doubt the patient, positive activities of commerce and industry, to which England devoted herself at the beginning of the eighteenth century, had the same effect.

In our own times the type has been even more sharply defined under the stress of new ideas. In the first place, as its traits have become clearer, it has been accepted as an ideal. For its special virtue is strength, moral strength, strength of character and will, the first of values in this modern and commercial England, where life and the struggle for life have become so intense, where success is only possible for those who maintain their faculties of attention, judgment and decision under so much that makes for fatigue and disquiet. English literature of the nineteenth and twentieth centuries shows us finished incarnations of this ideal, such as George Eliot's Tom Tulliver and George Meredith's Tom Redworth. But as a rule the artist is hostile to it, and emphasises its perversions in satirical portraits or caricatures, as Dickens did in his Gradgrind and Dombey, the author of Mark Rutherford in some characters of his *Autobiography*, and but yesterday, Galsworthy in his Forsytes.

Another idea helps to shape the type on the same lines. It is of aristocratic origin. The more democratic England becomes, the greater, it would seem, is the prestige of the type dominant under the ancient oligarchy : the gentleman—every one to-day thinks he has a right to the name. Now the gentleman was originally the squire, the autocratic master in his estate and parish, described in innumerable novels, from Godwin's *Caleb Williams* to Meredith's *Egoist*. He is a leader, a man of trained will, the master of his nerves, sparing of speech and gesture, for the guiding principle he received from his forefathers, the instinct which has been confirmed by education and by his very surroundings, is that he must never betray his passion and emotion—never *give himself away*. In the Soames Forsyte we have mentioned, born in the commercial middle class, but educated in an aristocratic school, the practical and the patrician ideas are combined : to be silent, to repress oneself, in order to be strong and give no opening to one's rivals ; not to flinch under a telling blow, but to preserve the mask of impassibility,

226

and thus conform to the recognised social pattern. However different in origin, however unconscious and undefined their motives, the two commandments are one in their teaching; the principle is always self-control.

There is a further reason for its acceptance. It agrees with the deeply-rooted sense of the conditions of health natural to the English: the health of the soul as of the body, of the individual as of society. Their instinctive attention to this is evinced by our neighbours in their peculiar social rules and methods of education; their insistence on long hours of rest in childhood, to ensure future endurance and steady the nerves; the importance they attach to open-air games; their contempt for outbursts of sensibility, for the contagious disorders of emotion, for brooding and melancholy, in general for all that borders on the eccentric and the excessive. It shows itself, moreover, in the strict convention which banishes dangerous realities from literature, and forbids exploration of the dark, disquieting depths under the surface of life; in the almost automatic power of customs and habits, the distrust of analysis and criticism, the attachment to established forms. Each generation, for instance, accepts the ready-made order of the Constitution and the forms of religion, for in these the English soul, unwilling to enquire what is left or perhaps what is no longer left of its faith, is still bent on finding support and guidance. Everything, indeed, in England seems directed to one secret end: that of preserving the enduring unity of the person and the group from the disintegrating influences of intense life or over-daring thought.

In this respect England has long remained distinct from the rest of the world. Whereas in other countries, man, in the course of the last century, under the influence of literary and social romanticism and the effect on nerves and brain of modern civilisation, has become more and more complex, unstable and sensitive (compare the vibrations of a Debussy, a Monet, a Goncourt, the dissonances of a Wagner, the fitfulness of a Schumann, with the steady, regular forms and serene strength of an earlier art), life in England has ever tended towards health and balance, at least in those classes which come under the plastic and disciplinary influence of English education. What an advance in this direction from the age of Byron to that of Tennyson, from that of Dickens to that of Kipling ! The success was so great, the regular, impassive, strong type was produced in such numbers, it assumed so perfectly the aspect of a magnificent and flawless automaton, that a reaction set in. Weary of this display of health and certitude, the new novelists and moralists conspire to attack it, and oppose it as champions of nature.

The movement is in a way a return to Shakespeare. For if the national type is very remote from those that now prevail among the less disciplined, more intellectual and highly-strung Continental peoples, the contrast is even greater when we think of that which obtained among our neighbours in the happy days of the Renaissance, when souls were so free. Of all possible forms of man, it would seem that there could hardly be two more dissimilar than the modern Englishman and the characters presented by the great poet.

II

It will be said, no doubt, that he was a poet, and that in modern England men are governed by a practical, and therefore prosaic ideal.

But there is poetry of a practical kind, a poetry of the will and conscience, which is, perhaps, essentially the most vehement of all. The virtues prized above all others in Victorian times were sung by Tennyson in forms almost too perfect ; and he himself embodied them. The idea of order, the conviction that there is no beauty, health or dignity outside voluntary obedience to a law—in short, a system of Puritan ethics, streaked with stoicism, inspired him and such prophets and moralists as Carlyle, Ruskin, Kingsley, as it was afterwards to inspire the vigorous poet of the Jungle and its Law. In like manner, in an age when English Protestantism was more literal and more ardent, Milton's organ-notes translated, as the Hebrew poets had already done, the secret enthusiasm of a soul self-contained, upheld by a single and sublime emotion, uncompromising in its absolute faith, strong and grave by virtue of its very limitations and its unchangeable form. It is the paradox of Taine's great book to present Shakespeare and Milton as two incarnations of the English spirit. True, he noted the difference between their respective periods, in other words, between those prevalent ideas, which work so powerfully upon man and multitudes that types and society vary as they vary.

The soul and the poetry of Shakespeare are, indeed, the opposite of what we find in the great Puritan poet. He is not will, but imagination, a multiple and multiform genius, a volatile flame escaping from the limits of personality, and transmuted into a thousand souls. His most general trait is spontaneity ; in him reason is not set up as the sovereign spiritual judge. His intellectual world is one of startling intuitions, where the hidden depths of man and life are revealed in lightning flashes : a world of soaring dreams, shifting sensibility, fantastic wit and irony ; a world of changes and contrasts, where the mind turns suddenly from the vision of a certain tragedy and impending fate, to the indifference and laughter of men and nature. A world of improvised music, rising in ecstasy to the highest ether, with incomparable swiftness and liberty of movement.

This aerial movement is what strikes us at once in Shakespeare. The power of Tennyson's rhythm lies in its patrician calm, of Milton's in its religious and almost Latin gravity ; Shakespeare's rhythm is as swift as Shelley's, and almost rivals it in fluidity. It hurries along like the chequered play of light and shadow on sheets of water. And this supreme ease of the verse informs the whole of the poet's creation. It seems as if it had arisen spontaneously, without any effort of directing and co-ordinating thought. Everything in it belongs to nature, not to law, and this is also the

main trait of Shakespeare's characters. They are not
governed by the conventions and codes of constituted
society. Primitive energies stir them, often destroy
them. Their passions run splendidly riot. The
Shakespearean world is a jungle without a law, more
perilous and greater than that of the later poet; it
is England perhaps, but England prior to essentially
English culture, an England amazing indeed, but in
reality less strange, more human than that of to-day,
because natural, instinctive, unfettered as yet by the
discipline that makes for order, conscience, reticence
and will.

In short, it is the world of the Renaissance, when
the moral climate was hotter and the human fauna of
Europe different; when the individual was bigger,
more vehement, less deliberate in act and vision; when
feeling was violent, tending either to manifest itself
immediately in sudden and complete action—may be
murder—or to reverberate within, diffusing itself in
a tumult of images and emotions—may be madness
—sometimes in a combination of the two, as in Hamlet
and Macbeth. Does not Hamlet, made, to all seeming,
for dream and meditation, confess: " Yet have I something in me dangerous " ?

Who can say what were the influences that worked
so powerfully upon the energies of man in our western
world at this period ? And who can analyse the
mysterious laws which govern the alternations of
fervid activity and long torpor in the different human
families, the shifting of the centres of civilisation, which
pass from east to west, from south to north, from one

group of nations to another ? We hear, no doubt, of the intoxicating effect of great discoveries (but why this outburst of invention ?)—antiquity, exotic worlds, the first perspectives of science, the endless magics and possibilities of art and beauty, the might and the marvels of nature. Inspired by the sight of the new realms opening out before him, man threw off the swaddling bands of the Middle Ages. In that spring-tide of Europe, in a world where all seemed new and splendid to him, his virgin and long dormant sensibility awoke under the new breath that came to him from the depths of space ; a warm life rose within him, and put forth luxuriant blossoms.

In Italy, where life turns more towards the outer world, where human beauty is modelled in light against a noble background of architecture and landscape, it was the corporeal presence of the new man that was apprehended, and enthusiasm expressed itself in plastic works. Among the English, whose senses are less quick and subtle, and with whom the spiritual world is paramount, interest centred in the soul, and drama, which follows its movements and interprets its pathos, was the great English art of the Renaissance. But in the England of Elizabeth and Shakespeare, as in the Italy of the Medici and Michelangelo, whose fertilising radiance eventually reached the misty island ; in the figures of painters and sculptors, as in the souls created by the poets, the same general influences of the period produced these common characteristics : strength, amplitude, liberty of life, an unbridled expansion of the individual. How clearly the affinity is seen in certain of Shakespeare's tragedies and comedies! How he divined the Italy of his day, the perilous anarchies, the graces and splendours of Venice and Verona! How naturally his heroes bear the beautiful sonorous Latin names!

Southerners or Northerners, they are primarily men of the Renaissance. They evince not only its great traits : exuberant vitality, ardour of temperament, youthfulness of thought closely akin to sensation, laden and a-quiver with images, like a tree with its spring blossoms, suddenness and excess in passion (their love, hot, violent, carnal, is hardly English), but also the secondary tendencies and manners, the outcome of education and fashion. They have the habit (so distasteful to the modern English) of expressing all their emotions, as if delighting in them, until the moment when the simple word or the cry of nature is wrung from them ; they incline also to hyperbole, to magnificent metaphors, to loaded ornament and verbal flourishes : conceits and witticisms decked out with classical and mythological allusions. Finally, they have the grand manner. The kings are truly kingly. A Hamlet has all the hauteur, irony and courtesy of a prince of the period. He does not live on the same plane as lesser men ; it is an act of grace when he comes down to it for an Horatio. Behind all these masks we guess at an Essex, a Southampton, a Pembroke, a Rutland. Our gallants wear their doublets of velvet and brocade, their ruffs, their long-embroidered gloves, all the stiff and sumptuous bravery which suggests the splendour of certain insects.

Here—with the Bohemia of actors and poets, his familiars of the Globe and the Mermaid—we have Shakespeare's world : that highest, lightest and most unstable portion of English society which the Italian radiance of the Renaissance touched and gilded. He did not belong to that other England, denser, deeper and more obscure, then stirred by the concentrated fervours of the Reformation. He appears to have known nothing of it ; there is no trace of it in his work, save three or four possible allusions to the Puritans, who must already have been of some importance under Elizabeth, for the Sunday closing of English theatres dates from her reign. Never were two worlds at once so close and so far apart, and after all, the whole difference must be referred to the governing ideas in each : in the one the idea of free beauty, in the other the idea of duty and law. In their action upon life and manners each produced a type as unlike the other as a species to a species—in fact, as Shakespeare to Milton.

Such a contrast sheds not a little light on the true causes and nature of types—those types which, when they have been established for some length of time, are deemed unchanging and abiding, and declared to be irreducible.

III

Not only did Shakespeare belong to a different civilisation, which fashioned the human substance differently. But in his work, and in what it shows us of himself, we recognise the traits of a certain race, a race undoubtedly an essential element, perhaps the

most important, in the people we call English. For
from the ethnic point of view, England is not simple ;
she tends more and more to make a distinction between
her Germanic and Scandinavian strains, and the Celts,
the descendants of the aborigines—not only those of
Ireland, Scotland and Wales, who would not allow
themselves to be called English, but those of the west
and south-west of the island, from Cumberland to
Cornwall, who have never claimed any special nation-
ality, who speak but English, and yet show physical
and moral traits which are considered British in the
more limited sense of the term. True, there are no
actual frontiers dividing indubitable Northmen and
Anglo-Saxons from the populations which are looked
upon as really indigenous. But if we traverse the
country from the North Sea to the Bristol Channel,
we shall note a change in the proportion of the two
types : the big, phlegmatic individual becomes rarer
as a smaller, darker species abounds, a species livelier
and more expressive. The eyes, however, are still
blue : dark hair and blue eyes are said to be a Cymric
combination. The psychological difference is no less
evident. Certain movements and tendencies of workmen on the Clyde or in Wales are explained by our
neighbours in a phrase : "They are Celts."

The current idea in England is, that this race has
given to the nation the majority of its artists and poets,
and that if the other, slow, silent and steady, was the
masculine force of the country, whose history and
success it determined, this sensitive variable race
represents the feminine element. Feminine is the word

Renan used to define the characteristics of the Celtic genius, and the Celts he was speaking of were precisely and exclusively these, the Celts of Ireland, Cambria and Cornwall, and consequently of Brittany, for our Bretons were a swarm that came from overseas in the sixth century. They are peoples apart, enclosed for thousands of years in districts which had scarcely any communication with the rest of the world, driven to the extreme points of those islands and peninsulas where the influences of nature are so special, and everywhere the same. Moist winds from the Atlantic, pale mists in which the world dissolves like a ghost, the uncertain sweetness of fine days, the endless dreariness of the " black months," the long-drawn, languid summer twilights, the ceaseless play of spindrift, the enervating onslaughts of storms : any one who has lived in these western outposts knows how such influences, if long-continued, act upon the soul, disturbing the regular flow of its vital energy, subjecting it to sudden tensions, to alternate states of passion and dream, enthusiasm and depression. No doubt the Breton or Briton countries tend to sensitise ; they induce a certain latent neurosis. Man in these regions is unstable, impressionable, strangely susceptible, prone to ponder, even to enjoy his melancholy. However sturdy the physique, the face, a certain hollowness about the mouth, betray a delicacy, perhaps even a weakness of the soul. The gaze is veiled and introspective ; it has a mournfulness which subsists even under the extravagance of the Irishman. *We are a sad-eyed people*, said one of their painters to me.

SHAKESPEARE

It is, of course, too much to attribute to this race nearly the whole of the poetic element in English literature, as is the fashion to-day. Generally speaking, there has been a fusion of Anglo-Saxons and Celts, except in the extreme east and west of the island, so that any soul expressed in a literary work has the dual origin. And besides, when we speak of races, we deal but with average or dominant traits, characteristics maintained only by the persistent mass and internal currents of a certain human group : isolate the individual, plunge him into a *milieu* where other magnetic currents prevail (as in the case of immigrants in America), and you will find new forms appearing after two generations. But during all the centuries of the old world, in Britain, where provinces remained separate and conditions of life unchanged, distinct types were able to endure, especially in the more remote regions. We should also reckon with the sudden reappearance of ancestral qualities in the individual.

This is why, throughout the history of English prose and poetry, we can recognise and follow a certain spiritual lineage, the persistent trait of which is a singular kind of dream, a dream tinged with a certain madness, so entirely divorced is it from the realities of earth, so illogical, aerial and wonderful is the world it pictures, as if by some magic incantation ; a world in which things seem strangely expressive, full of mystic meanings only to be guessed at. More or less it is the world of the old Mabinogions, full of music the soul alone can hear—a world where Love and Fate reign, where Nature, alive, and, as it were, spontaneously ordered, whispers to man and gives him signs and tokens. Those who would understand the kind of unsubstantial and mysterious vision I am trying to suggest need but recall certain names and certain creations of literature and art, the Malory of the Arthurian legend, the Spenser of *The Faery Queen*, the Shakespeare of *A Midsummer Night's Dream*, the Blake of the *Songs of Innocence*, the Keats of *The Eve of Saint Agnes*, the Shelley of *Alastor* and *The Sensitive Plant*, the Coleridge of *The Ancient Mariner*, the Tennyson of *The Lady of Shalott*, the Meredith of *Richard Feverel*, the Hardy of *Tess*, the Barrie of *Peter Pan*, Turner's ethereal landscapes and fantastic irradiations, Burne-Jones' knights and maidens, his strange backgrounds, rhythmical as a chanted spell, and in general the whole art of the English pre-Raphaelites. This kind of vision the contrast will help them to realise if they think of works of a very different complexion, those, for instance, of Defoe, Hogarth, Fielding, Constable (we might add, of George Eliot and Arnold Bennett), works almost Dutch in character, slow and sometimes heavy in their patient realism, setting down trait by trait all the individual detail of a soul and a figure—or again, those of Milton, Byron, Carlyle, the Brontës, Kipling, where imagination is supreme, but violent, charged with stormy energy, heaving, as it were, with passionate movements from that innermost self where will and personality centre.

The dream we are here trying to suggest is something infinitely gentler and more radiant; it is associated with a very different spiritual mood : passive, as under the influence of music, and hovering between joy and melancholy—changeful, as under the influence of love, and drifting between melancholy and joy. But it is often broken by capricious bursts of high spirits—dance, nonsense, singing, lyric poetry—such as glance or carol from the pages of Shakespeare's comedies or Meredith's novels. One might quote less shining examples, for the fancy that sports in this ideal radiance is not limited to a few rare artists. It is widely diffused ; we recognise it in a hundred expressions of popular art, in the literature of the nursery, for instance. In no country is this richer, more absurd and charming ; it abounds in tender dream-stories, such as *Peter Pan* or *Alice in Wonderland*, showing a world of topsy-turvey-dom ; in refrains and ditties where the images of the sheepfold and the fields rise without any logical connection, where the only sense is in the rhyme and rhythm—absurd rhymes, bewitching rhythms, of ancient, unknown origin (*Bo-Peep* is in Shakespeare), that sound like charms thrown to children by fairies. The old *mammow koz*, the grandmothers of our Brittany, sing just such lays and lullabies to the little ones. Think, again, of the Christmas pantomimes, which delight grown-ups as well as children, with their garlands of fruit and flowers, their choirs of girlish figures, floating on gauzy wings to a cloud-kingdom. And again of the frenzied reels and jigs of the Highlands and the Celtic countries, the mad capers, the drollery, the mock-solemn pirouetting of the clown. Remember the strange mood expressed in certain folk music—in those songs of Ireland and Wales where the yearnings of regret and desire intermingle with the feeling of the Past and of the Nevermore, with dreams of the Beyond, with mysterious " tears rising in the heart " as when we look across the dim sea in the northern twilight at an emigrant ship dipping below the horizon. And finally, the spiritual element, the pale, chaste apparitions, the dreamy quality and symbolic intentions of the art beloved of the public—all, in short, that sings and dances and floats and dreams in Britain, all the sweet, fantastic, unearthly things that astonish a reasonable Frenchman, as if in the midst of the hurrying commercial crowd of London he should suddenly light upon the cold, frail, visionary figure of an Ophelia.

This is the magic light which, piercing the smoke of factories, still irradiates the gray and black of an England disciplined for prose and action. Nowhere has it shone more vividly than in that unique kingdom we call the Shakespearean world. This kingdom is in all places where springtime, flowers, moonlight, lovers and poets are to be found. Brilliant, melancholy Watteau is one of its princes. But to know its true colours, those imagined by Shakespeare, one must have seen these fairy plays dancing and fluttering upon an English stage. Highly developed logic, studied and self-conscious art, excessive intellectual civilisation hinder such free movements, which seem those of Nature herself expanding into poetry as the life of the tree into blossoms. They demand the spontaneity, the flower-like freshness, the innocent, dreamy eyes, the unbound hair, the parted lips, all the fragile angelicised grace (*Angli Angeli*) that reveals itself in the sudden

SHAKESPEARE

dancing flights of children and young girls in that land.

The Shakespearean world: the very phrase is a kind of spell which lifts us from earth, and shows us the legendary forest of Ardennes, unreached by the tumult of the world; we listen to the peace filled with the twitter of birds, so sweet to the tired heart that we close our eyes to drink it in. In the green shade, where fir tree and olive link their boughs, the banished Duke smiles on his courtiers: shepherds, poets, nobles in the garb of Robin Hood. Jaques, the sentimental philosopher, weeps over the innocent wounded doe (*poor dappled fools!*) or ponders ironically on the follies of men. This fantastic Monsieur Melancholy bandies sighs and salutations with Signor Love. Rosalind in disguise, with mock dignity of masculine reason, undertakes to cure Orlando by her banter, whilst dreaming of kisses. Meanwhile songs float upwards here and there, like larks from a flowery meadow, shedding over the whole poem the joy and freshness of an English spring. Anon all the questing lovers find each other; they gather in couples, and their rhymes interlace and answer each other: alternating ditties, variations on the eternal theme, which make us smile by their repetition and extravagance, like the exaggerated gestures of passion in a pantomime dance. Then we have the shimmering spaces, the azure depths of *A Midsummer Night's Dream*, the swarms of sylphs, the fairy lullabies, the graces of Master Pease Blossom and Master Mustard Seed, the swoons of Titania, the genial braying of Bottom, the tender human couples attracting and repelling each other under the influence of the magic flower. Or we watch the frolic dance of fairies and trolls around the sleeping Falstaff, or see Jessica dreaming on a grassy bank in the moonlight. Now come Windsor and its gossips, Messina and the sparkling sword-play of Beatrice and Benedick, their gibes at love, and the final victory of love. Then *A Winter's Tale, Twelfth Night,* all the fanciful scenery of those comedies with charming titles of proverb or legend. And to end the Shakespearean insubstantial pageant, after all the superhuman dreams and terrible visions, after Othello, Lear, Macbeth and Hamlet, we have Prospero's final incantations, his farewell to his talismans, the dying music of departing Ariel, and, last, supreme picture in the solitude of the enchanted island, the amazement of Miranda, ignorant of the human world, at the radiant apparition of the prince—and then her ecstasy, her silent tears, the ineffable reality of life revealing itself : that life we have seen shaking under the lightning flash, and dissolving into darkness—and the rapture, at its virginal summit, of the two eternal beings in the eternal dawn of love.

The marvel in these fairy plays is their lightness, the winged swiftness of the vision, the airy, translucent character of the forms called up ; they are like white wreaths of dewy mist dissolving under the first rays of the morning sun ; the images conjured up by Shelley, his women, flowers and landscapes, are floating radiant phantoms of the same essence. How delicate and flexible this poetry, how changeful and iridescent the feeling that informs it ! Melancholy is linked with joy,

242

emotion with humour, tenderness with petulant wit. And throughout there is the deliberate choice of the improbable, the poet's defiant negation of common sense, experience and reason, his unencumbered soaring into an ideal world where all is " as you like it " and the impossible is not banned. Over this aerial world sparkles the star that danced when Beatrice was born.

By all these features the Shakespearean fantasy differs from those Germanic fables, even the most ancient, where the sense of mystery is profound, but undisturbed by any sudden flights, where wonder is passive and almost religious, where the soul does not disport itself in nature, but withdraws to meditate upon it, and drink in its vague, pantheistic influences. It differs more especially from those where, as in the pictures of the elder Breughel, fairies, dwarfs, devils, kobolds present the special traits and life-marks of a complete individual, each fixed in its peculiar form and character : a cunning, cruel, spiteful, or friendly spirit, inhabiting a solid body, in a world wonderful indeed, but dense and serious, and taking part in adventures subject to the laws of logic and almost real in their precision.

The difference here is akin to that we have noted between a certain kind of English poetry and works of a slower, more moral and realistic art. (Meredith and Matthew Arnold would have called them Anglo-Saxon.) The reason is, perhaps, that Shakespeare was born not a hundred miles from Wales, on the banks of that river Avon, which our Bretons would call Aven. It would be too much to enrol him under the Celtic banner ; but

---

at least German professors should not be allowed to annex him as one of their race—if indeed their race be unmixed. Were it possible to know those of his ancestors who lived in the sixth century—there may have been thousands of them—surely we should find more Britons than Saxons among them. One thing is certain: the chief characteristics of Shakespeare's poetry are of the kind the English consider especially Celtic. Is it not remarkable that among the great writers of their language, the Welshman, Meredith, is nearest to him by the intense life of his creations, by the truth, the logic, the depth of his psychology, however arbitrary and even fantastic the situations—by the lightning quality of his wit, by his freaks of fancy, his vivacity, the suddenness and loftiness of his lyrical flights? In the last of his novels, the title of which suggests the theme, Meredith contrasts the plastic imagination of the Celt and the stubborn, concentrated energy of the Anglo-Saxon.

Concentrated energy is not the quality we discern in the little we know of the poet himself. He was *the gentle Shakespeare*, one of those who inspire more tenderness than respect: *my Shakespeare*, says Ben Jonson, who was his friend—" sweet swan of Avon," probably a soul not very strong of will or capable of resistance. For so much flexible sensibility, such a gift for transmuting oneself into many forms are not consistent with a firm moral structure. Love seemed to him a malady, an intoxication impossible to resist, a fatal enchantment, destroying all reason, all power of self-command and self-guidance in the sufferer. *Poor worm, thou art infected,* says Prospero to Miranda — and this is the mournful theme of his most charming comedies. Such was certainly his own experience. Under the spells of Mary Fitton he was Antony in the little hands of Cleopatra. Antony, Romeo, Jaques, Posthumus, Macbeth, Hamlet, all these living characters he did not take from actual life but drew from his own self, to unburden himself—how they embody the same soul in its changing moods, at different stages in its disorder! A fitful, many-sided soul, powerless for action, devoid of enduring will and vigour, because too easily invaded, possessed and driven by dreams.

IV

Thus, whether we look upon him as mainly a Celt or mainly a child of the Renaissance, Shakespeare still seems very remote from the Englishmen we know. Yet he is English, intensely English, if we take the word in its general acceptation among foreigners, the meaning it has for every one in France when we speak of the English people and the English genius. The fundamental quality of his work, passionate imagination, informs the whole of English poetry—an imagination no less intense in the time of Browning and Swinburne, or of Keats and Shelley, than in that of Shakespeare ; and if this quality has become less evident in English life, it is probably because the modern social code forbids its manifestations. The contrast between the English of the Renaissance and those of to-day is not, as one might think at first, that between two distinct faunæ, but rather that between Nature and law, between the disorder born of excessive liberty, and order—one might say health : the health achieved by obedience to rules gradually accepted as the rules of moral hygiene. Now such progress cannot change the essential characteristics of a mind. For its degree of balance, form, and resistance is variable. We may see it weakening, and the whole personality disintegrating under the stress of disease. What cannot change is a certain structure of that mind—that is to say, certain aptitudes and tendencies. Its thought is made up either of direct images, with their swift appeal to emotion, or of abstract representations. It is either intuitive or analytic, living in the present, or in a world of ideas and feelings which it elaborates ; its vision of things is either disinterested or distorted by the promptings of passion or will, the reactions of a vehement and over-responsive *ego*.

Now the quality most often apparent in English literature is precisely this : a predominance of concrete imagination and of sentiment over logical thought, and we might say also, of spiritual over sensual activities. It is a lyrical element, strange as this may seem when we think of the more obvious England of sport and business—the element to which is due, together with the unquestionable supremacy of English poetry at all periods, the soaring flights and unrivalled emotional power, not only of the sixteenth century drama, but of the nineteenth century novel. One might quote every masterpiece of their literature if one wished to

show the persistence of this element, and the natural
importance among the English of that inner life
which their modern system of education and their
social ethics tend to make more intimate still by
suppressing its outward manifestations. Familiarity
with English poets and novelists makes us realise how
essentially French literature was formerly a logical
expression of general ideas, and how, during the last
century, it has become an artistic and colourful interpretation of sensation; in other words, how in both
cases it has dealt but with psychological events which
do not permanently belong to our deeper self. Henry
James, who knew and loved France, has noted this
last trait—I think in connection with Loti; but no
doubt he had also in mind the Goncourts, Flaubert,
and even Hugo, as compared with their English
brethren, from Byron to Carlyle and Browning.

It is, of course, difficult to prove truths of this kind
in words. But to suggest them, it may be enough if
we recall certain characters in English novels well
known in France, Kipling's Dick Heldar, for instance,
whose inner life, with its fervid yearnings and impulses,
seems to become more intense in the gloom and solitude
of his blindness, until the whole of his silent effort is
intent on controlling and concealing his despair. Even
before he becomes blind, the bulk and activity of the
inner world are so great in this artist that the outer
world vanishes under the crowd of haunting, disquieting
images which his eyes seem to follow. His pictures are
visions, sometimes his own, full of spiritual and mysterious meanings, like the works of those English painters

whose art is mainly poetry—his *Melancholy*, for instance, whose misery is expressed in a heart-rending laugh—sometimes those of an Edgar Poe, a seer of the same race as himself. Of course, such a character is extreme—extreme after the manner of a Lear or a Macbeth, for it proceeds from the same kind of imagination.

But now let us take a type of the opposite kind, the most prosaic and matter-of-fact imaginable, the Clayhanger Bennett has described for us in three novels, with an art akin to photography, telling us everything about his childhood, his family, his neighbours, his friends, his printing business, his marriage and his home, whilst suggesting the dingy background of bricks and the heavy, smoke-laden atmosphere of the Five Towns.[1] The author has tried to show us the average, contemporary provincial Englishman, who spends two-thirds of his days over figures or amongst machines, and has never dreamt of change, or even of a pleasure. Such a narrative is the epic of a soul, with all its hidden sub-conscious life, its infinite reactions to tiny daily events—minute in our eyes, but to the man himself of capital importance—with its shortcomings and inadequacies, but also with a certain beauty in its wealth of feeling, its virile strength of will and faithfulness, its slow, unique love-blossoming, checked as the rising sap in a tree might be by fire or frost, and suddenly resumed after an interval of ten years, and culminating in a supreme moment of happiness. And then, in the last volume of the trilogy, we see the slow return of that soul, through endless

[1] *Clayhanger, Hilda Lessways, Those Twain.*

secret anxieties, to prose and reality, the lesson of patience and tolerance it learns from its new life, and finally, its wise and happy effort to adapt itself to another soul.

In such novels as these, all that outer world which the Goncourts, Daudet, Huysmans would have described in terms of carefully studied art, is much less important than the invisible life of the characters. Events here are reduced almost to nothing ; they interest us only in so far as they act upon the mind whose intermittent growth they help us to realise. We get an impression of the successive moments and changes of a man, of the mysterious and fateful unfolding of a certain human life through time, as upon the screen of the cinematograph. We watch the growth of a germ till it becomes a plant, and are amazed by the abundance and delicate detail of the spiritual element. George Eliot had told stories of the same kind, as slow, epical, and fully-developed, stories of purely moral happenings ; and in them she had made us see not only the secret pathos of very ordinary lives, but the truth implicit in Shakespeare's greatest dramas : that character is fate, and that all destiny turns upon the discord or the harmony between two principles : the innate tendency of any given soul and the pressure brought to bear upon it from without. The lesson of *Hamlet* all the great English novels of our time repeat ; they are the out-come of the same faculty—the gift of psychological insight, the power of creating individual and complete souls, and developing them according to the logic of life. Of this power, the supreme examples are of course to be found in Shakespeare ; but it is also to be felt in the whole English theatre of the Renaissance. Accepting Brunetière's theory, we might almost say that when the dramatic form was atrophied under the constraint of Puritanism, the peculiar native gift from which it sprang was deflected to the novel—its successor and counterpart in the nineteenth century.

Thus the faculty that was at its highest in Shakespeare has ever been alive, and we generally find it combined, as in the dramatists of the Renaissance, with pathetic and lyrical powers which the modern writer is more careful to chasten and restrain. Poetic ardour and a deep sense of psychological truth : those two traits have always characterised English literature.

How are we to explain this dual tendency, save by the very abundance of that spiritual life which is the chief and constant object of art and observation in England —that intensity, which in some cases borders on morbid dream and passion ? Such a conception will seem a paradox to those who know the English but from outside, who remember only those they have met in hotels and on steamers—all those who seem but too healthy, whose conversation is confined to current anecdotes, whose gestures are apparently all according to rule, and who, at the age of cares and responsibilities, can find pleasure in pushing a little ball from one hole to another on the grass for hours. But let us not forget that in this country, the inner, the real man differs greatly from the visible social man—education and opinion directing the former to mask himself behind the latter. If we are acquainted with Mr. Galsworthy's

Forsytes and Pendyces, with Meredith's Austen Feverel, with Dickens' Dombey, we know how such souls may prey upon themselves without any change of outward bearing. Let us also remember that the original reason of this discipline is not only an aristocratic idea of form and etiquette, but a strong though obscure instinct of the conditions of health. True, that as a result of the *régime* of sport and open air life enjoined by this instinct, by the effect also of lifelong, self-imposed attitudes, the external man tends, in many cases, especially in the upper classes, to become the whole man. But nature has a way of asserting itself, and if manners repress it so strictly, it is because it is felt to be dangerous. The excess of power in the English soul—those capacities for dream, sentiment and passion so richly manifested in poetry, drama and the novel—may develop into a general and latent principle of disorder. Of this the English are aware when they speak admiringly, not only of the reason, but of the balance and essential healthiness of the French mind : " French sanity." Their social code is necessary to them ; away from it and from the surroundings that enforce its rules, the individual is apt to become abnormal. Again, this may seem a paradox, but it is no true contradiction to define the Englishman now as a creature of the hive or the flock, intent on copying his fellows, now as an extreme and eccentric individualist—and thus he used to be defined by all nations who knew the Englishman only outside his native sphere.

The eccentric individual still abounds in England,

sometimes isolated, and inspired either by mere caprice or by a systematic desire to act in contradiction to established manners, and hurl defiance at convention and society—remember Byron, remember Meredith's Lord Fleetwood—but more often affiliated to others of his kind, in clubs and societies—an inventor of new moral tenets, of new religions, of new ways of living— a Suffragist, a Christian Scientist, a reformer and saviour of society, an open air orator, an indefatigable apostle of the idea that possesses him. This type is more especially of the mystic and religious kind ; the sects which began to multiply in the sixteenth century have never ceased to produce it ; and it matters little if the faith which fires him directs itself—as in Shelley's case—against faith. He occurs frequently in novels, notably in those of Dickens, and Meredith's admirable Nevil Beauchamp, rapt in his humanitarian dream, indifferent to the happenings of real life, and utterly oblivious of self, is a finished example of the species.

These are the " oddities." But with others, a sudden shock, grief, prolonged solitude, over-strenuous conditions of life will upset the balance. Sometimes they become over-sensitive, and the will weakens ; more generally the inclination to dream throws off the restraints of reason, and the image in the mind develops, strangely growing and veiling the outer world. The man follows it, passive and hypnotised, with eyes that see things we cannot see. It may be a certain contemplation that finds in everything suggestions of terror and mystery, a contemplation the danger of which Lady Macbeth points out when she exclaims

SHAKESPEARE

Consider it not so deeply . . .
. . . These deeds must not be thought
After these ways ; so, it will make us.mad.

It is an element of disease, as in Macbeth and Hamlet
—of madness, perhaps, as in Lear ; but also, as in all
Shakespeare's over-intense characters, an element of
intense poetry : lyrical, metaphysical and religious
poetry, for the tumult of emotion remains within,
inspiring purely spiritual activities that support and
prolong one another—dreams, ideas, sentiments,
intuitions. It does not spend itself outwardly in
sudden gestures, as with the man of the south.

Such states are not rare in real life ; we find them
more especially—as in Shakespeare's drama—in people
hard pressed by necessity, hunted, driven. The moral
armour given by education, the social defences have
fallen away : the naked soul appears trembling before
a world which has become all solitude, shadow, terror
and tragedy. Now and again English newspapers
publish the will of some poor wretch who has drowned
himself in the Thames, or else the confession of a
criminal ; sometimes, in connection with a trial, a
letter of hopeless passion ; and the height of pathos
is reached. The man speaks then as if he saw his life
receding and detaching itself from him ; he is alone
before the abyss, before his Judge, or before an all-
absorbing vision ; and in the fever of such an hour,
emotion expresses itself in accents sometimes heart-
rending, sometimes full of a strange solemn peace that
seems already to have left the world behind. I remember such a letter, written by a youth who had killed

his betrothed and was sentenced to be hanged; justice is still strict and biblical in England. He saw her again as Tennyson's unhappy hero sees the pale, fixed, haunting face and closed eyelids of her he has lost " growing and fading and growing " upon him. Of his crime he wrote not as of a deed of ungovernable passion, but as a necessary, predestined act. He had killed out of love, with love, that the girl who had betrayed him should not live impure; he thought of her as purified by death; now he felt only worship for her. Some of his words recalled Othello's when, with breaking heart, he looks upon the frail white corpse of Desdemona. (*Pale as thy smock! . . . Cold, cold, my girl! . . . I kissed thee ere I killed thee.*)

If we wish to understand this eager acceptance of suffering, this tendency to torture oneself with haunting images, not at a moment of crisis, but in the course of an apparently quiet life, we should read the auto-biography of Mark Rutherford, a poet of whom fate had made a London clerk. Under the harsh rule of a hard taskmaster, he sat with others in a basement office for ten hours a day filling ledgers, endeavouring to turn himself into a machine, and dreaming all the while of the country, sick with repressed sentiment and imagination, and dying slowly, like Keats' captive eagle, pining for the sky. To find similar states of mind we must turn to men of an infinitely more passive type, who, yet, have never learnt to control themselves; we must go to the other end of Europe, to those Slavs of whom we are continually reminded when we begin to probe the English soul. Only these two peoples have that quality of the imagination which may be called *visionary* and is often expressed in the eyes. We saw it in Chaliapine's when he was acting Boris Godounov, that Slav Macbeth, who has supped full with horrors (there is something of Shakespeare in Moussorgsky, as in the creator of Raskolnikoff). A mystical look too, as if the palpable world had vanished and an unspeakable reality were revealing itself. Here, perhaps, we may find an explanation of the many strange sects which have swarmed in Russia as in England. The British Government found during the war that it had to reckon with its Doukhobors.

In Russia the abnormal element we are speaking of is evident enough. Should its existence among the English be questioned, we need but recall the visionary fervour of their Puritans, Shakers, Methodists, Salvationists, the collective frenzy of the great Revivals. Remember also that most of the phenomena and documents of Spiritualism and telepathy come from England, that many of that country's manors and woodlands are still haunted by ghosts like the Shakespearean stage. And again remember how persistent are the obsession of mystery and the presentiment of the supernatural throughout English literature ; note the solemn, fantastic radiance that enwraps certain tales by Kipling, by Dickens, certain poems of Poe (who was of pure English stock), of Coleridge, Shelley, Blake. Milton's infernal figures, his Satan himself, are bathed in it, and in their vaporous immensity take on the strange aspect of superhuman spectres. It is the light in which Tennyson's prince saw in sudden flashes the substance of things dissolve and felt himself the shadow of a dream. Such, too, was Carlyle's constant vision of mankind and the universe : a phantasm, a procession of phantasms emerging from darkness only to be engulfed in it again. Either intermittently or chronically all the writers we have mentioned are seers ; the faculties shown in their works are the opposite of reason, that is to say, of what we hold to be mental health. Some of them, Poe, Cowper, Swift, for instance, were certainly unsound. No wonder they excelled in painting strange or extreme states of mental or moral life, the paroxysm of emotion, those crises and tempests of the soul in which it finally founders. The literature of the people who, more than any other, now worship health has painted more power-fully and persistently than any other those disorders in which the internal forces of man, losing their balance, are seen in all their tragic grandeur.

This is the very kingdom of Shakespeare, from whom each of these poets seems to derive by one trait or another. All the powers they possess in a greater or lesser degree—the lyric gift, the haunting sense of moral realities, of a mysterious other world, concrete imagination and visionary dream, psychological insight, deep and dramatic intuitions of the dangerous energies latent in the human soul, under the calm surface of reason and civilisation—all these are included in his, the sovereign power. Taine judged it to be this last trait—the power of depicting the hidden depths of the soul unhinged by calamity—which constitutes the supreme grandeur of Shakespeare's drama. In Taine we may, no doubt, find a trace of that romanticism the poison of which he denounced, but had tasted. In the Shakespearean creation he admired a work of intuitive imagination, not of reason—still less of that classic reason whose virtues he has praised, though he has so often shown its limitations. He was, moreover, a psychologist, and his analysis of the mind, which included observations in the Salpétrière,[1] had led him to conclude that man is mad by nature, and that perception of the external world partakes of hallucination. The work of the great English poet confirmed all his conclusions. Not only was it not a product of reason, but reason appears in it as unstable equilibrium, unreason as the natural state to which man ever tends to return. Here psychology proceeds from pathology.

This, it may be objected, is too technical a point of view, that of the specialist who admires the poet's sudden and intuitive insight into the object he himself has methodically studied. But the object here is simply man, the internal essential man, so that the special point of view merges here into the general, human point of view, which is also that of the dramatist. For real drama is psychological, and its power depends on the degree of truth in the painting of souls, and on the intensity of their tragedy. Now what is this tragedy but the disaster that assails them, the shock they receive from it ? the greater and more powerful to stir our terror and pity, the more deeply

[1] The great Parisian hospital for the treatment of mental disease.

we see it working in them, shaking them with suffering and emotion, and perhaps overthrowing them altogether. It is a fact that suffering and emotion make for disorder and disease. They attack reason and will, gradually or suddenly disintegrating them, and setting in motion the automatic play of impulses, images and dreams. We may prefer other subjects, a drama where all is social discipline and intellectual perfection, noble and restrained speech, delicate gradation, well-knit and finished argument. We may, in fact, prefer order to violence and civilisation to Nature.

But however perfect such an art, its dramatic effect will be less powerful. For since tragedy is in souls, the more violent and deeper its effects upon the soul, the greater it will be—and to reach its climax it should go as far as the complete overthrow of the soul. And all should happen in accordance with the logical and secret processes of Nature and life. In a Lear we must first be made to feel the age and temperament of the king, the fitful impatience and tyrannical weakness of an impulsive, sensitive and passionate old man. We must recognise the immediate effect of the first blow, the sudden havoc wrought by the attack, as if an oak tree withered by age had been rent by the first stroke of an axe to its very base. We must be shown all the repercussions of the shock, the fever, the increasing rush of thought and gesture, the trembling of the white beard, the sudden, furious departures, the automatic returns of the old king, brought back as in a dream by the idea that rouses and possesses him. Mark the birth of madness, the strange and almost solemn terror of the man who dimly feels it rising within him :

Not mad, sweet Heaven ! . . . I would not be mad !

And then the second attack, the growing wildness of passion let loose, with the sudden intervals of calm : a tense and terrible calm, as in the centre of a cyclone :

> *I will not trouble thee, my child ; farewell.*
> *We'll no more meet, no more see one another.*

What pathos in the incomparable scene on the storm-swept heath, when Lear's madness has declared itself, when the old man raves in darkness and solitude, and the fool throws in his ironic comments! Then, after frenzy, the calm of exhaustion, with whispered, almost childish words, marking the ruin of the will,— the soul now a passive, sentient thing, nothing of the world remaining for it save Cordelia's loving, soothing presence—that presence which is like a gentle hand laid on an aching brow :

> *. . . Come, let's away to prison ;*
> *We two alone will sing like birds i' the cage :*
> *When thou dost ask me blessing, I'll kneel down,*
> *And ask of thee forgiveness. So we'll live,*
> *And pray, and sing, and tell old tales, and laugh*
> *At gilded butterflies . . .*

And to finish it all, the father's absorbed, obstinate contemplation of the dead girl, as he kneels beside her, remembering nothing but the voice which used to bring peace to his heart :

> *. . . Her voice was ever soft,*
> *Gentle, and low,—an excellent thing in woman.*

Nothing but this memory, and the deadly sense of
the Nevermore, when the old heart breaks at last
between slow, soft words, of such intensity !

> . . . *Thou'lt come no more,*
> *Never, never, never, never, never !—*
> *Pray you, undo this button : thank you, sir.—*
> *Do you see this ? Look on her,—look,—her lips,—*
> *Look there, look there !—*
>
> [*Dies.*

More purely psychological still is the drama in
Hamlet—a drama not of action but of inaction—the
excess of thought and imagination in the prince, his
constant tendency to spend himself in ideas and images,
paralysing his faculty of action, so that the tragedy
resolves itself into this : the gradual disorganisation of
a given character by the haunting idea of a certain duty
of which it is incapable. And this story of a soul is so
poignant because it is so inevitable and true. The
apparition and words of the ghost have shaken to its
foundation the noble, meditative spirit, lonely from the
first, absorbed in grief and suspicion, whose weakness
is not at once manifest :—note the terse precision of
his cross-examination of Horatio and the two soldiers
as to what they have seen. The effects of the disorder
are immediately evident in his incoherent speech, his
gesticulation, and half crazy laughter. The rest follows,
brought about by psychological necessity, the more
apparent because Shakespeare took care, in *Hamlet*
as in *Lear*, to place side by side with the more tragic
hero a secondary character (Laertes—Gloucester),
whose situation is the same, but whose drama is

different, simply because the soul structure is different.
But in Macbeth, the murderer, a disposition and a
disease closely akin to Hamlet's are seen again ; the
man is weak, a dreamer, given to brooding, still more
a prey to his fancies, without defence against imperative suggestions. See how those thrown out by the
witches take hold of him—and then the fixed idea is
born, grows, and at once absorbs and isolates him. See
his subjection to a stronger will. Lady Macbeth
scolds him as if he were a child, urging him forward
straight to the deed : a deed beyond all that his
nerves and his imagination can endure. For this
murderer is a poet. All that he feels, dreads after the
crime, when he comes back to the vast peace of night
and listens to its infinite silence as he had listened,
haggard and motionless, to the fear of the two grooms
(*listening their fear*)—all that he dreams when he looks
at his bloody hands, whose red " plucks out his eyes,"
and seems to him to be overspreading the world, all
that startles him when he hears the distant screech of
the owl, all this is, no doubt, the beginning of disease,
but also the most tragic and mysterious poetry. It
inspired Musset, and nearly the whole of Maeterlinck's
dramatic work echoes the obscure, breathless emotion
of this scene.

Such a man is not only a poet ; he is a seer. In
Macbeth, as in Hamlet and Prospero, we find that
strange faculty of metaphysical insight which we
have seen manifested at various moments of English
literature. Under the rapt gaze of the chieftain who
did violence to his own nature when he killed, and of

the prince who must do violence to his in order to kill, as under the meditative gaze of the magician, the reality of things vanishes, and over the Shakespearean drama we recognise the spectral light Carlyle saw flooding the vistas and multitudes of History. Man is a passing shadow, life a brief flame kindled and flickering for a moment between two voids : a phenomenon, a mere form the substance of which is ever passing ; and what is this substance itself but a phantom ? Time is a shoal emerging from a boundless ocean. The world is woven of the same stuff as our dreams. As the spirits called up by Prospero have melted into air, together with all the baseless fabric round them, so the great globe itself and all which it inherits shall dissolve, and leave not a rack behind. But if all things disappear into the gulf, all things ever return from it ; as in Shakespeare's drama, when Hamlet and all the protagonists are dead, the curtain does not fall ; we see life going on, a new order, new fates arising. The abyss is not empty ; we feel an unspeakable and solemn reality ever present there : the fateful Power that governs all tragedy.

Here, then, opens the dark unfathomable deep— that of which the mystery has always haunted men. We feel it, see it everywhere behind the poet's passing show. All the dreams of his creatures culminate in the endless dream each race has peopled with its own figures and symbols, which the Puritans had begun to identify with their idea of the biblical God and his rigorous law. This particular God does not appear in the poet's work ; his dream is more general, yet not purely metaphysical ; it is religious, because it is interwoven with that emotion, that tremulous yearning for the infinite and the eternal (*there's nothing serious in mortality*), that craving for justice after all the injustices of earth—also with that melancholy and weariness (*this world-wearied flesh*), that quest for the meaning of life and death which have never ceased to inspire the thought and the poetry of England, and which are the living elements of her religion. It is to the honour of this people that from the beginning they have been more deeply concerned than others with the mystery of things. It is a noble trait in man to be disquieted by this mystery. Because, like our Pascal, Shakespeare probed it so anxiously and persistently, he speaks to all men, and the most English feature of his genius is also the most human.

THE END.